The Pocket Mentor for Video Game Writers

Want to become a writer in the games industry? Then this is the book is for you. Award-winning game writer Anna Megill provides all the essential information and guidance you need to understand the industry and get your foot on the ladder.

The book explains in simple, clear language exactly what a beginner needs to know about education requirements, finding job opportunities, applying for roles, and acing studio interviews. Professional writers will learn how to run a writers' room, manage a team, create documentation for various project phases, and navigate studio politics.

The Pocket Mentor is designed to be a just-the-facts companion to *The Game Writing Guide: Get Your Dream Job and Keep It*, but it stands on its own as an invaluable go-anywhere resource for beginners and seasoned pros alike.

Anna Megill is an award-winning game writer and industry veteran with experience writing primarily for modern AAA games. In her nearly two decades of game development, Anna has worked for some of the top studios around the world, such as Ubisoft, Arkane, Remedy, and Square Enix. A longtime advocate for marginalized voices in games, she provides resources and advice to aspiring writers through her website. Anna currently works at Playground Games on their upcoming Fable game.

The Pocket Mentors for Games Careers Series

The Pocket Mentors for Games Careers provide the essential information and guidance needed to get and keep a job in the modern games industry. They explain in simple, clear language exactly what a beginner needs to know about education requirements, finding job opportunities, applying for roles, and acing studio interviews. Readers will learn how to navigate studio hierarchies, transfer roles and companies, work overseas, and develop their skills.

The Pocket Mentor for Video Game Writers
Anna Megill

For more information about this series, please visit: http://www.routledge.com/European-Animation/book-series/PMGC

The Pocket Mentor for Video Game Writers

Anna Megill

CRC Press
Taylor & Francis Group
Boca Raton London New York

CRC Press is an imprint of the
Taylor & Francis Group, an **informa** business

Designed cover image: Kina Lee

First edition published 2024
by CRC Press
2385 NW Executive Center Drive, Suite 320, Boca Raton FL 33431

and by CRC Press
4 Park Square, Milton Park, Abingdon, Oxon, OX14 4RN

CRC Press is an imprint of Taylor & Francis Group, LLC

© 2024 Anna Megill

Library of Congress Cataloging-in-Publication Data
Names: Megill, Anna, author.
Title: The pocket mentor for video game writers / Anna Megill.
Description: First edition. | Boca Raton : CRC Press, 2024. |
Series: The pocket mentors for games careers
Identifiers: LCCN 2023024216 (print) | LCCN 2023024217 (ebook) |
ISBN 9781032252476 (hardback) | ISBN 9781032252452 (paperback) |
ISBN 9781003282259 (ebook)
Subjects: LCSH: Video games--Authorship--Vocational guidance.
Classification: LCC GV1469.34.A97 M444 2024 (print) | LCC GV1469.34.A97
(ebook) | DDC 794.8/3--dc23/eng/20230602
LC record available at https://lccn.loc.gov/2023024216
LC ebook record available at https://lccn.loc.gov/2023024217

ISBN: 978-1-032-25247-6 (hbk)
ISBN: 978-1-032-25245-2 (pbk)
ISBN: 978-1-003-28225-9 (ebk)

DOI: 10.1201/9781003282259

Typeset in Times
by SPi Technologies India Pvt Ltd (Straive)

For Nixy

Beloved writing partner and stern critic for nineteen years.
I miss you.

Contents

Acknowledgments   xvi
List of Abbreviations   xvii

Meet Your Mentor   **1**
Note   3

1 The Basics   **4**
What Is Game Writing?   4
What Do You Mean by Game "Narrative"?   4
How Is Game Narrative Different from Regular Narrative?   5
    Player Agency   5
    Perils of Player Control   5
Are There Different Kinds of Game Writing?   5
What Does a Game Writer Do?   6
    Don't Writers Just Write Dialogue?   6
What's a Typical Day for a Game Writer?   7
    The Three Ps   7
    So Game Writers Do *All* the Narrative Stuff?   7
What's the Difference Between a Game Writer and
Narrative Designer?   8
    Narrative Specialties   9
What Are Other Narrative Roles?   9
How Do I Become a Game Writer?   11
    The Reality of Game Development   11
    It Gets Better   11
Notes   12

2 Wise Up   **13**
What Skills Do I Need?   13
    Baseline Narrative Skills   13
    Spreadsheets   14
    Pitching and Presenting   14
    Tags and Conditionals   14
    Communication and Collaboration   14

Do I Need Any Specialized Skills?   15
     Voiced Dialogue   15
     Characterization   15
     Screenplay Software   16
     VO and Mocap Direction   16
     Writing Skills   16
     Design Documentation   16
     Game Systems Knowledge   16
     Implementation   17
     Perforce   17
     Programming   17
Do I Need to Know How to Program?   17
Do I Need a College Degree?   17
What's the Best Degree for Game Writing?   18
Do I Need to Go to a Game College?   18
What If I Can't Go to College?   18
     Extremely Online   19
     Internships   19
Can I Teach Myself Game Writing?   19
What's the Most Important Thing to Learn?   21
     Steps to Success   21
Notes   21

3 On the Hunt   **22**
How Do I Break into Games?   22
Isn't Finding Work Just a Numbers Game?   23
     Keep Your Day Job   23
How Do I Make Myself Hireable?   23
How Do I Make Contacts in the Games Industry?   24
     Social Media   24
How Do I Make Connections Offline?   25
     Conventions   25
How Do I Find Work with No Industry Contacts?   26
     Spec Apps   26
How Do I Find a Job?   26
     Studio Career Pages   27
     Recruiters   27
     Staffing Agencies   27
How Do I Know it's a Good Place to Work?   28
Is This Job Right for Me?   29
Notes   30

4 Introduce Yourself **31**
Am I Qualified for This Job? 31
   Title 31
   Education 32
   Experience 32
   Skill 33
How Do I Read This Job Post? 33
How Do I Apply for a Job? 34
What Do Recruiters Look For? 35
When's the Best Time to Apply for Jobs? 35
When Should I Nudge the Studio? 36
Should I Reapply for a Job? 36
What If the Answer Is No? 37
Should I Ask for Feedback? 37
What If They Won't Give Me Feedback? 37
Do I Need to Write a Cover Letter? 38
   The Short Answer 38
   The Long Answer 38
What Makes a Good Cover Letter? 38
How Do I Write a Good Cover Letter? 39
   Extra Credit 40
What Should a Cover Letter *Not* Say? 40
P.S. Relax 41
Note 41

5 Resume Speaking **42**
What Makes a Good Resume? 42
What Should a Resume Include? 42
Where Do I Find a Good Resume Template? 43
What's the Best Resume Format? 43
   Content 44
What Are the Dos and Don'ts of Resumes? 46
   Do 46
   Don't 47
   Especially Don't 47
Do I Need a Resume Service or Career Coach? 47
What's a Keyword Pass? 48
How Do I File My Resume? 48
How Do I Write a Resume Step by Step? 49
Note 49

6 Showcase Your Work   **50**
  Do I Need to Show Writing Samples?   50
  What Samples Should I Send?   50
    Fill the Brief   50
    Interactive Work   51
    The Rules   52
    Contextualize!   52
  What Should I Not Send as Samples?   53
  How Do I Submit Samples?   53
  How Do I Make an Interactive Portfolio?   54
    What's Your Story?   54
  What Goes in My Public Portfolio?   55
  What Goes in My Private Portfolio?   55
  What Do Studios Look for in Portfolios?   57
    PROSE   57
  How Do I "Tell My Story"?   58

7 In the Spotlight   **59**
  What Is the AAA Interview Process Like?   59
  What Can I Expect at Each Step?   60
    The Screen   60
    Hiring Manager Interview   61
    Follow-Up Interview   61
    Team Interview   61
    Studio "Panel" Interview or Onsite   61
  How Do I Prepare for an Interview?   62
    Know Your Stuff   62
    Mock Interviews   62
  What Are Interview Dos and Don'ts?   63
    Do   63
    Don't   64
  What's an NDA?   64
  Should I Sign This NDA?   66
  How Can I Tell If I Passed the Interview?   66
  What Are the "Next Steps"?   66

8 Time to Shine   **68**
  What's a Writing Test?   68
  Why Do Studios Have Writing Tests?   68
  Should I Take a Writing Test?   69
  What If I Don't Take the Writing Test?   69
  Can I Get Paid for the Test?   70

What Does a Writing Test Look Like?   70
What Do Studios Look For?   71
How Can I Tell If It's a Scam?   71
   Red Flags   71
How Do I Ace the Writing Test?   72
   Do Your Research   72
   Follow the Instructions   73
   Don't Cheat!   73
   Minimize Risks   73
   Have Fun!   73
What If I Bomb the Writing Test?   74
   Ask for Feedback   74
Can I Use My Tests as Writing Samples?   74
How Do I Turn Tests into Samples?   74
   File Off the Serial Numbers   74
   Stay Inside the Lines   75
Notes   75

9 The Dotted Line   76
What's in an Offer Letter?   76
How Do I Know it's a Good Offer?   76
   Salary Information   77
   Cost of Living   77
   More   77
How Do I Negotiate a Better Offer?   77
   Never Go First   77
   Know Your Worth   78
   Negotiating Bias   78
Should I Work for Exposure?   78
What Salary Should I Ask For?   79
   Make A Budget   79
   Find Your Floor and Ceiling   80
   Shoot Your Shot   80
   If They Say No   80
   If They Say Yes   81
Do I Need a Lawyer?   81
What's a Reasonable Rate for a Lawyer?   81
What Should I Look for in a Contract?   81
   Is Everything We Agreed on Here?   81
   Is Anything I Don't Agree with Here?   82
   Clauses to Watch Out For   82
   Unreasonable Clauses   83

Can I Work on Side Projects?   83
     Deed of Variation   83
Signy Sign   84
Notes   84

10 Press Start   85
What Should I Do on My First Day?   85
What Should I Do My First Week?   86
How Do I Know What Work to Do?   87
What Is Preproduction Work Like?   88
What Is Production Work Like?   88
What's a Writer's Day to Day Like?   89
How Do I Work in a Writers' Room?   90
How Do I Get Heard?   90
How Do I Deal with Imposter Syndrome?   91
How Do I Get to the Next Level?   91
     Get Direction   92
     Training   92
     Mentoring   92
     Keep Improving   92
Notes   93

11 Hurdles   94
How Can I Work in This Environment?   94
How Do I Overcome Writer's Block?   95
How Do I Ask for a Raise or Promotion?   95
     Procedure   96
     Performance   96
     Keywords   96
     The Next Level   96
     Get Feedback   96
How Do I Manage My Manager?   97
     Show Some Empathy   97
     Know Thyself   97
     Tactics   98
What If My Manager Won't Help?   98
Do I Have to Crunch?   98
How Do I Stop Burnout?   99
Help! I'm being Mistreated. What Do I Do?   99
How Do I Deal with Discrimination?   100
When Should I Go to HR?   100

How Do I Handle Studio Politics? 101
   Allies 101
   Enemies 101
   Find Your Community 102
Notes 102

12 Running the Show **103**
What Does a Lead Do? 103
   When You're the Lead 103
How Do I Keep Track of Everything? 104
How Do I Manage a Team? 105
Help! How Do I Manage My Time? 106
   Prioritize 106
   Assess & Adapt 106
   Delegate 106
How Do I Balance Creativity and Management? 107
How Do I Keep Up Team Morale? 107
How Do I Help My Team Through Crunch? 108
How Do I Run a Writer's Room? 109
Notes 109

13 Making the Team **110**
How Do I Put Together a Team? 110
   Assess Your Needs 110
   Make a Hiring Plan 111
What Do I Do as a Hiring Manager? 112
   Be Fair 112
What If I Don't Have Budget for Writers? 113
How Do I Create a Writing Test? 113
   Be Cool 114
How Do I Onboard New Writers? 115
How Do I Estimate a Line Count? 115
   Quick and Dirty 115
   Napkin Math 115
Notes 116

14 Document Everything **117**
What Is Narrative Drift? 117
How Do I Prevent Narrative Drift? 117
   Speak Their Language 117
What Documentation Do I Need? 118

What Do I Need for Preproduction?   119
   Defining the World   119
   Lay a Solid Foundation   120
How Do I Write a Good Story Pitch?   121
How Do I Write a Story Bible?   121
What Goes in a House Style Guide?   122
What Do I Need for Production?   123
How Do I Keep Track of the Story?   124
How Do I Prep for Recording and Mocap Sessions?   125
   Schedule   125
   Casting Materials   125
   Scene Counts   126
   Glossary   126
   Represent!   126
How Much Studio Time Do I Book?   126
How Do I Help Localization?   127
Notes   127

15 Exit Stage Right   128
When Should I Leave a Job?   128
How Do I Look for Work While Working?   128
   Start the Hunt   129
How Do I Show Work That's Under NDA?   129
What If I Don't Want the Job Offer?   130
I Want This Job Offer! Now What?   130
   Timeline   131
How Do I Leave on Good Terms?   131
How Do I Resign?   132
How Do I Write a Resignation Letter?   132
How Do I Guarantee My Game Credits?   133
What Work Can I Take with Me?   134
Should I Sign All These Papers?   134
What Do I Say in My Exit Interview?   136

16 On the Road   137
Why Can't I Work Remotely?   137
   Reasons for Being Local   137
How Do I Find International Work?   138
How Do I Plan for Overseas Work?   138
How Do I Pay for My Move?   139

How Do I Apply for a Visa?   140
    Biometrics   140
    Picking Up the Visa   140
Where Will I Live?   141
Can I Bring My Pets?   141
How Do I Choose a Mover?   142
What Should I Pack?   142
Do I Need to Speak the Language?   142
How Do I Handle Culture Shock?   143
    Change Your Mind   143
How Do I Network Abroad?   143
How Do I "Find My Community"?   144
Notes   145

17 Wrap It Up   146

Acknowledgments

This book would not exist without the kindness and support of my brother, Chris Megill. M.B. and Jan Kim, thank you for keeping the faith when I lost it. All hail Kina Lee for the fun cover image. Fist bumps to cool kids Ann Lemay, Eevi Korhonen, Lisa Hunter, Toiya Kristen Finley, Rhianna Pratchett, Josh Scherr, Mary Kenney, Eddy Webb, Clara Fernandez-Vara, Strix Beltran, Grant K. Roberts, Olivia Wood, Ed Stern, Ed Fear, Sachka Duval, Jill Scharr, Peter Fries, Alex Epstein, Steve Burnett, J.D. Sorvari, Chris Tihor, Jana Sloan Van Geest, Tara J. Brannigan, and Matthew Weise. Martin Lancaster, cheers for holding down the fort. Big thanks to the infinitely patient Will Bateman at Taylor & Francis. And a big shout-out to all the lovely narrative folks in The DIN. Thank you all for your wisdom, advice, and for cheering me on through a hard year of writing.

List of Abbreviations

ADO	Azure DevOps
AI	Artificial Intelligence
AU	Alternate Universe
BIPOC	Black Indigenous People of Color
CMoS	Chicago Manual of Style
dev	Developer
DIN	The DIN = The Discord for Interactive Narrative
DLC	Downloadable Content
EA	Electronic Arts
ECGC	East Coast Games Conference
ERG	Employee Resource Group
FAQ	Frequently Asked Questions
FOMO	Fear Of Missing Out
GaaS	Games as a Service
GDC	Game Developer's Convention
GDOC	Game Developers of Color
GenderEQ	An app that analyzes who speaks more in meetings
GIG	Games Industry Gathering
GWU	George Washington University
HR	Human Resources
IGDA	International Game Developer's Association
IP	Intellectual Property
IT	Information Technology
mocap	Motion capture
MVP	Minimum Viable Product (NOT most valuable player)
ND	Narrative designer
NDA	Non-Disclosure Agreement
NPC	Non-Player Character
NYU	New York University
PAX	Penny Arcade Expo
PTO	Paid Time Off
Q&A	Question & Answer
QA	Quality Assurance
RPG	Role-Playing Game

RPS	Rock, Paper, Shotgun
SIG	Special Interest Group
TOC	Table of Contents
UI	User Interface
US	United States
VO	Voice Over
VR	Virtual reality
WGGB	Writers' Guild of Great Britain

Meet Your Mentor

Hello, friend! You've picked up this book, so something about game writing must spark your interest. Is it the right career for you? Some of you are belting out a hearty "yes." You play games, you understand story, you're ready to go! Some of you are working writers, and you've cracked this book to make sure you're not missing any critical tips. But maybe you've never considered game writing as a possible career. Maybe you know the moving parts of a video game but have no clue how game writing differs from "regular" writing. That was me, when I first started out: curious, ambitious, but with no idea what a professional game writer does day to day. That's okay! By the end of this book, you'll know the essentials.

First off, game writing is fun. It's a rewarding and creative craft where you build virtual worlds out of words. It challenges your skills and tests the limits of your imagination. It's an immensely rewarding job, and I wouldn't want to do anything else. But be warned: game writing is also one of the most competitive jobs in an already competitive industry. Breaking in is a challenge. Staying in is even harder. Believe me, I know. I've been in the games industry for nearly two decades now, working for some of the top studios in the world. My projects have won many honors, including a few Game of the Year and Best Narrative awards. I've spoken at major industry events around the globe about everything from emergent storytelling to crafting an interactive portfolio. I've moved all over the map for jobs—with two international moves in one year! Right now, I live in the English countryside, working as the narrative lead for a AAA[1] game studio. I'm a working writer in the modern games industry, so I know the challenges you'll face. I know what studios want in a game writer. I know how to land jobs. As a manager, I know the entire hiring process inside out. I also know the daily challenges you face as a writer and what strategies work when collaborating with other disciplines to ship a successful game. I've been through it all, many times over.

But in my two decades of games industry work, I've never had a mentor. I always wanted one, but I never found the right person to take me under their wing and share their wisdom. When I faced a problem or opportunity, I had to find solutions on my own. I googled answers, bounced ideas off friends, and

DOI: 10.1201/9781003282259-1

fumbled together my own system for doing things. Too often, I ended up taking the hard path when there were easier ways. If only I'd known.

I dreamed of having an experienced game writer I could call for advice. When I pictured that relationship, it was always as a sort of apprenticeship. We'd have long conversations about The Industry and Game Narrative and my mentor would impart their sage advice to me across many years of individual instruction. Someday, I'd emerge a full-fledged master game writer ready to take up their mantle and teach an apprentice of my own. But you know what? That's not how mentorship works in real life. Those chats with friends I mentioned? That was mentorship. That desperate post on Twitter that a fellow writer answered? Mentorship. And as the years passed and writers started coming to *me* for answers, mentoring often took the form of quick chats about situations the writer was facing at the time. I tailored my advice to meet those specific questions and fleeting needs. Mentorship means helping someone in the thick of battle. It's not lofty, big-picture musings; it's practical, granular, and above all, immediately actionable advice.

This small book provides that kind of mentoring. It supplies the essential information you need to find and keep a job, from start to finish, from narrative hopeful to narrative lead. This book offers instructions for crafting application materials, from cover letters to samples. I whisk you through the steps of submitting a solid writing test and creating an interactive portfolio. I highlight the fine print of NDAs and contracts, and call out deal-breaking clauses. And don't worry! I won't leave you working writers hanging! Learn how to pitch and track stories, assemble your dream team, run a writers' room, ask for raises and promotions, and handle crunch and burnout.

Before scribbling this advice, I plowed through a stack of books about game writing as a craft. They were all either too abstract and high level to be useful, or nitpicky and fussy in a way that doesn't matter in the trenches. My book is a response to those guides. I pitched this book as an "anti-textbook" that offers quick, clear, and realistic advice. The language I use is deliberately non-academic and plain. It's a chat with a friend, not a lecture from an instructor. This book is also affordable for students and new writers. (This was important for me! I was broke as a joke when I first started out in games, so I know that books can be luxuries.) And the "Pocket" part of the title means something. It's a small book you can take wherever you go and find help fast.

Don't read this book cover to cover or study it like you're cramming for a test. Pull it out for specific situations in your career. Job interview in an hour? Ask your pocket mentor for last-minute pointers. Tossing together a portfolio? Grab a coffee and ask your pocket mentor about format. Hiring writers? Your pocket mentor's on it! That's how you should think of this book: snippets of off-the-cuff advice from someone who's been there. Many images are simple "napkin sketches" that I jotted out to clarify a point during real-life mentoring sessions, so you're getting the authentic experience.

I wrote a more detailed book, *The Game Writing Guide: How to Get Your Dream Job and Keep It*, that I strongly encourage you to read as well. That book explains the reasons and research behind my advice and offers wisdom from a collective of the top narrative talent in our industry. The books are designed to complement each other, so definitely pick up my *Guide* if you want a deeper dive into any topics. But this book has the quick-and-dirty, just-the-basics info you need to do all the things a game writer does.

So, approach the information in this book with that spirit. Imagine that you contact me to ask a burning question. We meet at a café and chat over a cup of coffee. You tell me what troubles you, and I respond. These are my answers, captured in text and drawings, and meant to get you over a hurdle and on your way fast. Are you ready? Then pop open the next chapter and let's go!

NOTE

1   Pronounced "triple A." These games are the equivalent of big-budget Hollywood blockbusters.

The Basics

1

Let's start at the beginning. Not the *very* beginning because I expect you have some experience with video games already. You probably know what an NPC[1] is and that they speak dialogue. You probably know what a game menu looks like and the purpose of a loading screen. And you may also know the basic components of storytelling: protagonist, antagonist, acts, plot, and so forth. But hey! If you have no experience with games or storytelling, that's okay too. I'll cover how to get the right education for game writing in the next chapter. Right now, let's run through the basics of game narrative. I'll use plain language for the beginners in the room, but honestly? It's not that complicated.

WHAT IS GAME WRITING?

In this book, when I say, "game writing," I mean the type of writing you find in video games. So game writing includes the story, characters, plot, and text that comprise a video game's narrative.

WHAT DO YOU MEAN BY GAME "NARRATIVE"?

It's the story the game tells. In big AAA games, this includes the main plotline (the big "story" of the game), and all the smaller side quests, conversations, and character moments you find along the way. It also includes the story told through menus, journals, shops, loading screens, signs, and even the world you travel through. Every part of the game that deepens your understanding of the story, characters, and world can express "narrative." I draw a distinction between "story" and "narrative" in this book to explain how the pieces fit

DOI: 10.1201/9781003282259-2

together, but you can use the two words interchangeably and no one will ding you for it. When in doubt, "narrative" is your cover-all term.

HOW IS GAME NARRATIVE DIFFERENT FROM REGULAR NARRATIVE?

At its fiery core, game writing means interactive writing. It requires active participation from the player, whether by clicking a mouse, pressing buttons on a controller, or through body movements in VR (virtual reality). I could go down the rabbit hole of "well, *actually*, all writing requires interaction in the form of reading or imagination" but this isn't that kind of nitpicky book.

Player Agency

You'll often hear game developers mention "player agency" in reverent tones. Good game writing melds with design to give players control over their game experience. Of course, it's impossible for players to get a story ending you haven't planned, but you can make them *feel* like they forged a unique path. For a better understanding of player agency, check out *The Stanley Parable*. It toys with the illusion of player control in clever (and funny!) ways.

Perils of Player Control

Game writing comes with a daunting set of challenges. When players can roam around freely in the game world, they might experience your story out of order or in circumstances you hadn't anticipated. Predicting the decisions players make so you can plan reactions to them is one of the most challenging aspects of interactive stories. But when you get it right, the world responds to players' every action and it feels glorious.

ARE THERE DIFFERENT KINDS OF GAME WRITING?

Yes! There's a nonfiction branch of games called "serious games" that focuses on education rather than entertainment. On the fiction side, there are three main branches:

- AAA games are the big-budget blockbusters. Some well-known titles are *Tomb Raider, The Last of Us*, and the *Legend of Zelda* games. These are the games I work on.
- Mobile or "casual" games are often played on the go with phones or tablets. Think *Candy Crush, Monument Valley*, or *Switchcraft*.
- Independent (or indie) games are made by smaller teams not affiliated with a big studio. Some successful indie games are made by a "team" of one person. (I salute you, *Stardew Valley*!)

Every branch has its own writing standards and requirements. Most AAA games have big, glossy cinematics[2] while mobile games may rely more on text and menus.

WHAT DOES A GAME WRITER DO?

When I started out in games, I joked that I wasn't a writer, I was a "rewriter," because my job was polishing lines pre-written by designers. That still happens at some studios, but most game writers create narrative elements from scratch now. Writers brainstorm plot and untangle story logic. We write the main, overarching story of the game, but we also tell the story of the world, the characters who inhabit it and express its culture, the things those characters say and do, the written elements of the world, such as posters, signs, notes, and letters—plus all the writing for items, weapons, outfits, and other UI[3] elements. Game writers also create materials for internal use by the studio. We write pitches, "story bibles," marketing copy, and newsletters. So, what does a game writer do? Everything with a narrative!

Don't Writers Just Write Dialogue?

Yep, some writers, especially short-term contract writers, are brought in specifically to write lines of dialogue. But even writing basic combat "barks"[4] requires understanding the characters, systems, and how they fit together into the story of the world. You wouldn't expect a dark elf in a fantasy game to scream, "Grenade!" or "On your six!" when you're fighting, would you? Of course not. Writers must tailor their work to the needs of each game so that even the simplest lines of dialogue feel organic and in character.

WHAT'S A TYPICAL DAY FOR A GAME WRITER?

It's a rollercoaster ride. Your day as a writer changes all the time, depending on a range of factors, from individual assignments to where the game is in development. One day you might brainstorm missions with designers and the next you're thinking of puns for "armor." You might write screenplays, crafting recipes, or UI text. Or you might spend the entire day entering hundreds of VO[5] lines from a spreadsheet into "buckets" of dialogue. (You'll spend more time working in spreadsheets than you can imagine.) Or you might read through feedback from a playtest. Or diagram a conversation. Or be in the mocap studio with actors, explaining motivations to help them deliver their best performances. Or you could spend the entire day in a conference room fixing plot holes. Even small tasks take more time than you'd think. It took months to find the perfect name for the Threshold Kids series. Most days are calm, but major changes can drop out of the blue. If you crave routine, you might struggle with the chaotic nature of game development schedules. Personally, I like the variety. It keeps things interesting.

The Three Ps

Snooze alert! Game writing isn't all swapping jokes in the writers' room. The bulk of your work isn't fun. To survive the dull bits, you need the three Ps: *Patience. Persistence. Passion.* I know the word "passion" raises hackles because some unscrupulous companies take advantage of it to exploit or underpay developers. But nothing's wrong with caring deeply about the work you do. Passion gets you through the boring tasks: Fixing typos. Updating the wiki. Revising, and revising, and revising. If you can't stay invested in your work and look past the day-to-day drudgery of the job, you'll be miserable.

So Game Writers Do *All* the Narrative Stuff?

As part of the Narrative team, yes! The capital-n Narrative team isn't just writers, it consists of narrative designers (NDs), editors, dialogue designers, story managers, narrative producers, and even some dedicated testing roles in QA.[6] Modern AAA video games have well-developed characters with arcs, backstories, and natural dialogue filling out a world with weather, a day-night cycle, politics, religions, and local customs. Writers and narrative designers collaborate with other teams to tell their story in a fully realized game universe. So, really, everyone on the team makes the game narrative.

WHAT'S THE DIFFERENCE BETWEEN A GAME WRITER AND NARRATIVE DESIGNER?

That's a great question! The line between these roles is famously blurred, but here's the key difference: only one of these roles *has* to write, by definition. The supporting structural work of the story can be done by either writers or designers—often by both. But if you're talking about pure writing like lines of dialogue, that's a writer's work. And if you're talking about pure systems, like the mechanics of delivering the story to players through dialogue, then it's likely a designer. Take a look at this picture of Socko the Clown (Figure 1.1).[7]

FIGURE 1.1   Socko the Clown as a Game NPC.

Game writing is WHAT the clown says ("Hardy har, stranger!") and narrative design is the mechanics of HOW he reacts: recognizing that you haven't interacted with him before and pulling an appropriate response ("stranger") from a small database of barks when you press X. Both roles might decide to make that character a clown, and both roles might decide where to place that clown in the game world. The disciplines are deeply intertwined. But here's a shorthand rule: writers are more concerned with plot, character, and lines of dialogue, while NDs work with game systems, implementation,[8] and the *delivery* of narrative information. That means narrative designers often help design the game features and systems that express the story. But honestly, I've held both titles in my career and found little difference in the work.

Narrative Specialties

Just to make things more confusing, each role has different specializations. Writers are scriptwriters, screenwriters, and plain ol' writers, but they're all different titles for essentially the same job. Narrative design, however, can be quite specialized. A "narrative features designer" defines in-game story features and collectibles, like the memory vaults in *Psychonauts*. A narrative design implementer enters narrative elements into the game engine and makes them playable. Other narrative design roles are more technical and specialized, but I'll keep it simple. In this book, writers own text and NDs own systems—with a lot of overlap in between.

WHAT ARE OTHER NARRATIVE ROLES?

The narrative umbrella shelters a bunch of roles. I won't describe them all here, but it's important to know how they all fit together. So the next page shows a bird's eye view of the narrative hierarchy (Figure 1.2).

You've got directors up top and entry-level narrative folks at the base. Studios like Valve have flat hierarchies, but most AAA studios are structured like a standard pyramid. Familiar, right? Responsibility follows the same hierarchy: the more experience you have, the more story ownership you get (Table 1.1). The top tiers are more about defining a vision and overseeing work than they are about keeping your hands in the creative material of games.

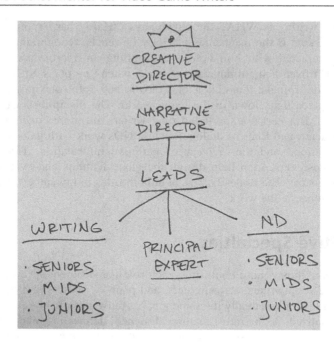

FIGURE 1.2   The narrative hierarchy.

TABLE 1.1   Narrative responsibilities by role

ROLE	RESPONSIBILITY
Junior	Learn! Your main job is to ask questions and learn as much as you can.
Mid	Create! Be an example for entry-level writers and NDs. Show them how you practice your craft. Be supportive, try not to dim the stars in their eyes, and help them navigate this strange new industry. And keep learning and growing yourself.
Senior	Feedback! Help mid-levels with their craft. Teach them what you know about interactive narrative, realizing a vision, creating characters, writing within systems, etc. You're their standard when it comes to craft, so help them shine. Here's where you'll start specializing and refining your skill set.
Lead	Mentor! Support your team on their journey. Keep them invested in their work. Don't let folks slip out of that leaky pipeline. Help your team learn specialized skills: How to collaborate with other teams for holistic work. How to estimate a line count.[9] How to map a character arc against the story. How to plan a narrative that works within existing systems and features. How to work with actors in a mocap studio. Share your knowledge and provide guidance.
Director	Inspire! Provide a story vision and help the team understand it. Show off their work and present the team in the best light. Be Narrative's liaison to the publisher and public. Fight for good story at the highest levels.

All these roles have more responsibilities than I can fit into a tiny table, but you see how your focus changes as you grow in seniority. Juniors think task by task. Directors need to galaxy-brain the narrative elements for the entire project and make sure it's all cohesive.

HOW DO I BECOME A GAME WRITER?

This is The Big Question! I'll spend this entire book answering it and will barely scratch the surface. There isn't an easy "fill out this form and we'll pop you in the next available slot" approach to becoming a game writer. It's a tough industry to crack, and the competition for narrative roles is intense. To break in, especially if you're starting at ground zero, you'll need knowledge, good communication and collaboration skills, a solid professional network, and patience on top of your writing talent. And even then, it's tough.

The Reality of Game Development

That brings me to my main goal as your mentor: keeping it 100. I love making video games, and I've had a long, successful career, but I'm one of the lucky ones. One of the privileged ones. The average career for a game dev lasts five years. I've seen talented writers come and go from the games industry. Some left to start families. Some burned out. Some found jobs outside games. The industry is a tough place to work. You've seen the headlines. You've read about the scandals. Gaming is no utopia. Every '-ism' you face out in the world exists here. In my decades as a dev, I've encountered most of the problems you read about: discrimination, harassment, abuse, crunch, burnout—the works. At one point, I left AAA for a while and worked on small, games-adjacent projects. But I missed video games and came back. And that's the crux of it. When making games is good, it's very good. It's so good that it outweighs all the bad.

It Gets Better

With every expose and headline, the games industry reckons with its problems. Progress seems glacial, but the games industry *is* getting better. So yeah, you'll have hard times. No question. I won't sugarcoat it for you. But if you can find a studio that values you and a project you love, nothing tops the feeling of playing a game you wrote alongside the fans who adore it. I want you to know that feeling. I want to help you create a career where you experience it. So, be realistic. Be prepared. And let's work together to find your space in games.

NOTES

1   NPC = Nonplayer character. Any character in the game not controlled by you.
2   Cinematics = in-game movies that develop the plot. Also called cutscenes or cines.
3   UI = User Interface. That's what we call all those menus in games: your inventory, storefronts, pop-up windows with information about loading or saving, all those boxes and buttons you interact with.
4   Barks are one-off lines of dialogue, like "Nice weather today!" and "Reloading!"
5   VO = voiceover. The voiced lines of dialogue in a game. They're often grouped into small collections or "buckets" by type and topic. A bucket of greeting lines, for example.
6   QA = Quality Assurance. These are the testers who find and report bugs in the game.
7   Clown vector art from Freepik.com
8   In its most basic form, "implementing" a design means taking the design plan or words on the page and entering them into the game engine (software like Unreal or Unity) so they become playable.
9   A line count is exactly what it says on the box. It's an estimated number of all the voiced and unvoiced lines of text in the game. I'll show you how to make one in Chapter 13.

Wise Up

2

Education doesn't have to mean traditional college or an expensive game design program. There are distinct advantages to those routes, but they aren't accessible for everyone. They're expensive. They're exclusive. And they're not realistic options for people in certain situations or cultures. So, what are your other options? Let's walk through them.

WHAT SKILLS DO I NEED?

We know that writers write and NDs design, but what exactly does that mean? What skills do they require? Unsurprisingly, the rock-bottom necessity for both roles is storytelling. You must know how to tell a compelling story. That means knowing narrative structure, characterization, exposition vs. action, and all that good dramatic stuff. It also helps to know the tricks for good interactive storytelling (versus traditional storytelling). How do you make a satisfying narrative branch? When do you use cutscenes over conversations? How long should a line of ambient dialogue be? Learn all the rules and constraints that go with writing specifically for games.

Baseline Narrative Skills

Here are some basic skills shared by writing and narrative design. Note that "writing" isn't on the list, but communication is.

- Storytelling
- Worldbuilding
- Communication & Collaboration
- Office suite (Email, Word)
- Wiki competence (Confluence)

- Spreadsheet software (Excel)
- Database competence (Jira, ADO)
- Dialogue tags and conditionals
- Pitch and presentation skills (PowerPoint, public speaking)

I call these skills the baseline because every good candidate has them. You likely have the first column of skills. Most people know how to send an email or make a blog post. But some of the other skills might take some study.

Spreadsheets

You'll spend a good chunk of your time as a game writer working in spreadsheets, so learn the basics. Nobody expects you to be an Excel world champion,[1] but know how to fill them out without destroying your producer's meticulous formatting.

Pitching and Presenting

Selling your story ideas to leadership and other disciplines is a critical skill for narrative folks. Know how to win people over to your vision with a presentation that speaks their language.

Tags and Conditionals

Currently, this isn't a hard requirement, but I think it will be soon. Some of the proprietary programs at AAA game studios let writers easily assign emotion tags ("this line is happy/sad/angry, etc.") and conditionals ("use this line if the player has finished Mission 2") to dialogue, so this task increasingly falls to them.

Communication and Collaboration

They're considered "soft skills" and therefore valued less, but they're the bread-and-butter skills of our craft. Writing is communication at its core. And game writing is collaboration, full stop. You can't tell your story without help, especially in AAA, so you must be able to work with others.

So, there you have it. That's what you should know before applying for narrative roles in games. Not so scary, is it?

DO I NEED ANY SPECIALIZED SKILLS?

Take a peek at my table of specialized skills for each discipline (Table 2.1). Aha! There's writing! It's a required skill for game writers but not necessarily for NDs.

Let's look at the game writing side of things first.

Voiced Dialogue

Many of you saw this skill and thought, "Pfft. I can do that." Many of you are wrong. There's an art to writing game dialogue. Lines must fit your narrative constraints yet still read easily and contain essential information. Many game writers fall into the trap of generic language, especially for lower-tier NPCs. Or they write lines that read beautifully but sound unnatural when spoken. Trust me, it's humiliating to watch an experienced voice actor struggle with your "clever" wordplay in the recording booth. You have to write for speech, not reading.

Characterization

Players remember characters, not plot.[2] So make them interesting!

TABLE 2.1 Narrative role specializations

GAME WRITING	NARRATIVE DESIGN
• Voiced dialogue writing	• Design documentation
• Characterization	• Game systems knowledge
• Screenplay software (Final Draft, Scrivener, Celtx)	• Implementation skills
	• Perforce
• VO and mocap direction	• Programming

Screenplay Software

Most modern games have movie-like elements that get written as screenplays. This format provides a common language for recording studios and actors, so it helps if you can write one. In-house AAA tools often mimic software like Final Draft and Scrivener, so if you're familiar with those programs you have an advantage.

VO and Mocap Direction

You might have a dedicated studio director for recording sessions and shoots, but not always! Sometimes you get called in to coach the actors yourself. Either way, you want a narrative person in the studio to provide clarification or the backstory. Or to help actors pronounce your fancy made-up fantasy names.

Writing Skills

So, there you have your specialized writing skills. Writers focus more on the content of the story: dialogue, character, and story at a textual level. You don't have to be a tech whiz to be a game writer. Some basic tech knowledge helps, but you can leave systems and design specializations to narrative designers.

Design Documentation

Game writers create story bibles and narrative designers create design documents. These are usually short, technical summaries of features and how they work. The documents are usually collaborations between narrative design and other disciplines. An in-game book, for example, requires help from UI/UX (to create the book template and pop-up interface), art (the book "asset"[3] in the game), level design (to place the book in the world), and writing (the title and contents of the book).

Game Systems Knowledge

A good narrative designer thinks of game systems as a tool in their belt. Your interaction with the Chaos System in *Dishonored* determines what ending you receive. Stealth is rewarded; carnage is not. The Nemesis system in *Shadow of War* gave your enemies a history and personality. But even a simple system like NPC greetings can do narrative work. Who doesn't feel a swell of pride when villagers shout an awed, "Look! It's the Hero of Shaemoor!" at you after your first big battle in *Guild Wars 2*?

Implementation

I mentioned that "implementing" a design means putting narrative information into the game engine. It can also mean placing narrative items or NPCs in the game world and making sure they "trigger" the way they're supposed to. Like pressing X to hear lines from our pal the clown in Chapter 1.

Perforce

This program is how assets get into the game. It's simple to use, as it's mostly a series of folders you check information in and out of. You'll have custom tools as well, but Perforce is ubiquitous at AAA studios.

Programming

I included this as a specialization because it's helpful and many NDs are able to do some light programming. Which brings me to my next point.

DO I NEED TO KNOW HOW TO PROGRAM?

Nope! The misconception that game "writing" is programming is so common that it's an industry joke: "Oh you write for games? What language, C++?" But there's no programming required. The better you understand game systems, the better you can express story through them, so it's useful to learn a programming language for that insight. But I know some game writers who can barely turn their computers on, so programming skills are pure icing on the cake.

DO I NEED A COLLEGE DEGREE?

This question is tricky to answer because, no, you don't *need* a degree. You need to know how to tell a story, through interactive writing and design. That means understanding how stories work, how to break down story patterns, and how to craft a compelling story from scratch. College isn't required for that, but formal education is still valuable. You'll learn skills and become part of a cohort that will offer you distinct networking advantages in the future. It's also much easier to travel abroad for work if you have a degree. And remember that scary statistic about five-year game dev careers? If you leave games for another field, you'll want a degree to get you started. So if you have the finances and opportunity to go to school, go.

WHAT'S THE BEST DEGREE FOR GAME WRITING?

An undergraduate degree ticks the box, while leaving your options open. A master's degree (or its equivalent) is also common among writers. But there's no reason to go for a PhD unless you plan to teach later on. Study literature, language, linguistics, screenwriting, history, drama, and any other subject that interests you. The important thing is learning how to express yourself on the page. If you plan to be a narrative designer, it's useful to know a few programming languages, but the studio can teach you tools and languages. The knowledge of how to craft an interesting story is the skill they expect you to bring with you.

DO I NEED TO GO TO A GAME COLLEGE?

Some schools have programs or tracks tailored for game writing and narrative design. Schools like NYU's Game Program or AU's Game Lab are rigorous and prestigious and you'll learn a lot, but you don't have to attend a games-focused school to be a game writer. I majored in English Literature and Computer Science at a traditional liberal arts college and learned everything I needed to know. Also, if you study at a games school, be wary of specialized programs with no narrative track. They tend to treat narrative like a "wrapper" for mechanics. That's not how game writers think of our craft.

WHAT IF I CAN'T GO TO COLLEGE?

For many people reading this book, higher education is not an option. You can't afford it, you're the caretaker or breadwinner at home, you have other responsibilities—there are many reasons why it might be out of reach. That's okay! You have other options.

Extremely Online

If you can't make it to a brick-and-mortar school, maybe online training is your answer. You can take classes online as part of adult education or extension programs at Harvard, Stanford, and GWU, to name a few. Also check out Udemy or your local college's continuing education annex. Game programs like Full Sail and the Academy of Art offer their curricula online too. Ubisoft sponsors the Pixelles Montreal Game Incubator, a two-month game workshop for women and BIPOC. And some professional writers teach seminars on everything from Gamewriting 101 to more advanced screenwriting classes. Most of the schools I listed have scholarships and funding available, so see if you qualify.

Internships

If you want to jump in and get work experience right away, some studio internships act as feeder programs and can lead to permanent hires. EA, Bioware, and Ubisoft all do this. Smaller studios like ArenaNet also have occasional internship spots that allow you to learn the basics of the role. Check company websites for internship possibilities—but be aware that they're as competitive as entry-level jobs.

CAN I TEACH MYSELF GAME WRITING?

Yes. Everything you'd learn in college you can learn on your own. There are countless books, papers, articles, and talks about game narrative a mouse-click away. We live in a golden age of information about game writing—almost too much information! Some of the advice out there is misleading or outright bad, so I wrote up a short guide of resources for you.

ANNA'S GAME WRITING STARTER KIT

- Start with these introductory books (Figure 2.1).
  Read the books in any order, but read them thoughtfully. They'll point you to other resources, so follow that trail! Check out your library to see what's available or pick up a copy online. Maybe pool your money with other writers to create a small, shared library.

FIGURE 2.1   Anna's game writing starter kit.

- Watch some industry talks: Go to the GDC Vault, AdventureX, and Develop:Brighton channels on YouTube and watch everything narrative related that grabs your interest. Jon Ingold's talk on "sparkling dialogue" is one of my favorites.
- Read the Writer's Guild of Great Britain guide to *Writing for Video Games.*
- Read Emily Short's blog.
- Get your mitts on Twine, Articy, Inkle, or some other game writing program and create an interactive story.
- Participate in game jams to learn collaboration and communication. Try the Global Game Jam as a starter.
- Join an online writer's group for feedback. The Discord for Interactive Narrative (The DIN) has a workshop channel where people can share their work and get feedback.
- Repeat as needed until you're ready to go professional.

Read all the theory you can get your mitts on and then make some games! Seriously, the best way to learn is to get in there and get your hands dirty. Make small games. Make Twine games. Collaborate in game jams. Start figuring out how to tell stories in an interactive way. Learn what works for you, what you like and don't like, and what kind of games suit your writing style best. Not only will your writing improve and your knowledge grow, but you'll have projects to list on your resume.

WHAT'S THE MOST IMPORTANT THING TO LEARN?

The most important step toward becoming a game writer is *practice*. Make games and get feedback on your work however you can. That cycle of writing – feedback –revision is where you'll see your work improve. *Get other people's eyeballs on your writing*. I can't stress this enough. It's scary to put your work out there for critique, and some people aren't kind with their feedback. But it's the key to getting better. This is where you'll learn to separate yourself from your work, learn what feedback to take on board and what to ignore, how to tailor work to someone else's tastes, and what motivates and excites you as a writer. Learning to give constructive feedback and receive critique is valuable in and of itself, but the best part of this process is creating solid work to submit as samples.

Steps to Success

To sum up this chapter, here are your steps to success:

- Study – whether at school or on your own.
- Practice – learn to write and revise.
- Polish – finish your work and put a gloss on it to create samples.

When you've done all that, you're ready to start your job hunt.

NOTES

1   Yes, Excel is now a competitive esport. Check out the *Microsoft Excel World Championship* https://www.fmworldcup.com/excel-esports/microsoft-excel-world-championship/

2   Tom Abernathy and Richard Rouse. "Death to the Three-Act Structure." GDC Narrative Summit 2014. GDC Vault. https://www.gdcvault.com/play/1020050/Death-to-the-Three-Act

3   An "asset" is any item that gets *added* to the game. An in-game library would be filled with book "assets." A narrative asset might be a note or line of dialogue. It's a way to quantify and track items that go into the game.

On the Hunt

3

As I write this chapter, headlines blare the news that another round of layoffs has hit the games industry. The job market is flooded with experienced developers who are fresh out of work. They join the job-seeking ranks of thousands of students who graduate each year, eager to enter the industry. And all of these people are vying for the same roles as you. How the heck do you find work in such a competitive job market? It's not easy! But it's not impossible. Let's break down the challenges one by one, starting with The Big One.

HOW DO I BREAK INTO GAMES?

This isn't the answer you want, so brace yourself: you might not. I started this book by warning that you've chosen a competitive industry. And the reality is that you can do every single thing right and still not break in. Luck and privilege absolutely play a role in landing game jobs. I won't sugarcoat that. I wish I had a magic formula for breaking in, but there isn't one. Anyone who claims they know The Way is lying. All you can do is try your best. Show people what you bring to the table and hope they appreciate it. And don't let the competitive market dishearten you! There are ways to improve your odds. Luck is a factor, for sure, but you can encourage luck to come your way. A valuable facet of networking is sharing your intent with people who can help you. Let the world know you want to be a game writer. Post writing that shows up in web searches, such as interesting, game-related blog posts. Create Twine or Inkle games. Create a public online portfolio. Write an article for a prominent industry site like Game Developer or RPS. Get your work out there where influential people can see it. And keep adding new work. It's good practice, in every sense. If you position yourself well, opportunities will come knocking.

DOI: 10.1201/9781003282259-4

ISN'T FINDING WORK JUST A NUMBERS GAME?

You've heard the saying: apply for enough jobs, and eventually you'll get lucky. "It's a numbers game!" people yell. "Law of averages!" Is this true? Well... Yes, in the sense that if you keep at it, eventually you might find work. But not if you submit the same samples, the same resume, the same application, over and over, and expect lightning to strike when it didn't before. If you keep learning, growing, and adjusting your application materials, then yes! It's true. Eventually, you'll land a writing job.

Keep Your Day Job

Securing your first game-writing job may take a while, so hunker down and prepare for the long haul. Keep your day job or another source of income while applying so you can support yourself. How can you focus on finding games work when you can't pay rent? A "money" job gives you a stable platform to launch from. And you never know! You might land your dream job right away and turn the money job into a side hustle.

HOW DO I MAKE MYSELF HIREABLE?

If you've studied as I suggested in the last chapter, you've already taken a huge step forward. Keep learning and improving the work you'll show studios as samples. That's the best thing you can do. Seize every opportunity to gain experience. But being a good writer is only part of what gets you a job. You also need to learn how to talk like a game dev and understand the work on a professional level. Watch interviews and conference talks as I mentioned before, but the best way to learn how to talk game dev is to...talk to working game devs. And the best way to meet them is by networking.

HOW DO I MAKE CONTACTS IN THE GAMES INDUSTRY?

Networking gives some folks clammy hands, but it doesn't have to be scary. Think of it as a chance to meet people doing something you're interested in. Most game devs are happy to talk about a shared interest, give advice, or chat about a game you both love. We're just ordinary people. So don't be intimidated and get out there and meet us. Don't worry. It's easier than you think!

MIND YOUR BRAND

You are your own brand, so mind your online presence. Future employers will google you. Curate search results so that you're projecting the image you want. Brand yourself however you want. You can be The Guy Who Makes Games About Pickles or the Biggest Claerith Shipper Evarrr! You decide what you want to be known for. I'm merely advising you to look at it closely so you're projecting what you want.

Social Media

The easiest way to find game devs is on social media. Pick your platform! Twitter was the best place for networking just a few months ago, but it's undergone changes since then and isn't The Place to Be like it was before. This is a pivotal moment for online networking, and I have no idea how things will end up. The safe strategy is to find developer friends on every platform. Remember all those devs you saw in the GDC videos last chapter? Look them up on social media and connect with them. Search #GameWriting on Twitter, join The Discord for Interactive Narrative, The GIG, or find People Making Games on Mastodon. LinkedIn is where the recruiters hang out, and you definitely want to meet them too.

Once you find game writers, connect with them. Here's my formula for making a good first impression:

- Follow a dev online for three weeks. Say nothing.
- Observe their interests and conversations. Notice the tone of their interactions.

- After three weeks, engage with them. Respond to a post or ask a question. Take your tonal cues from the interactions you observed. If you're respectful, you'll be fine.

Job posts are another reason to follow devs. Game writers share job openings at their studios and often have inside information about roles. Some devs collate big docs of job links and studio information, like the master list[1] that Jan David Hassel has assembled. Most devs are happy to answer a few questions about their craft, so ask! Ask for advice. Find out what their inspirations are. Let them know you're a fan. That's how you connect with people.

HOW DO I MAKE CONNECTIONS OFFLINE?

One easy way to make connections is to join a professional organization. Try one of these:

- International Game Developer's Association (IGDA)
- Writer's Guild of Great Britain (WGGB)
- Women in Games International (WIGI)
- Game Developers of Color (GDOC).

Join a special interest group (IGDA's Writing SIG is good) or join an online game writers' group on Twitter or Discord. Find local game jams and meetups. If your local scene's a desert, start your own group!

Conventions

There are gaming conventions across the globe. Try the Game Developer's Convention (GDC), Game Developers of Color (GDOC) convention, or smaller ones like OrcaCon or the East Coast Games Conference (ECGC). Most countries have their own regional gatherings. Everything from the Nordic Games Conference in Sweden, to GStar in South Korea, to Africa Games Week in South Africa, and Gaming Istanbul in Turkey. Note that conventions like PAX or Gamescom are more for fans than developers, so try to attend the industry-focused gatherings.

HOW DO I FIND WORK WITH NO INDUSTRY CONTACTS?

Having contacts in the industry helps, but you don't need them to find work. Narrative jobs are popping up all over the place these days. They're easier to find than ever before, largely thanks to centralized job databases. The best resource for open roles is currently GrackleHQ. It's free, searchable, and there's no registration required. Here are some other large job databases.

- Game Dev Jobs
- GI Biz's Job Board
- Remote Game Jobs
- XP Game Jobs

- Game Job Hunter
- Indiedb
- Hitmarker Jobs
- Game Jobs

Spec Apps

If you don't see any open roles at your dream studio, it's fine to ask them if they're hiring or not. Some places have open applications for that very purpose. But it's a gamble. Most speculative applications are dead ends. When I was first starting out, I pulled up the GameDevMap for my town and contacted every studio listed. I once sent thirty cold emails without finding a single possibility. Fortunately, there's a better way to do it now. I use GrackleHQ to learn about open roles, then visit the studio's site for more information.

HOW DO I FIND A JOB?

I'll walk you through this answer step by step. First, go to a job site. Let's use GrackleHQ for our example.

Keywords and Filters: The search keywords you enter will vary by role, but I get good results from the following terms: game writer, narrative, interactive writing, content writer, narrative editor, story designer, and worldbuilding.

Look at the search results and make sure they match your needs. Some points to look out for:

- Is the job remote or do you have to work on site?
- When was the opening posted? A job that's been open for a long time might mean the studio has high turnover, that they haven't found the right person yet, or that they're filling multiple positions with one ad. (A company might hire two senior writers with one senior writer job post.) Whichever option it is, that's valuable info.
- What are the role responsibilities? The title might sound like a good fit, but roles such as content writer, technical writer, and game writer do very different work. Which is the job you want?
- Choose a listing that interests you, read it, then visit the company's site to see if they have the same job posted there. Most AAA studios have an application form where you can apply directly to the studio.

Studio Career Pages

The best place to look for work is on the career page of the studio you want to work for. Companies usually post the job there first, with information about the studio culture and benefits packages. I recommend applying through the site whenever possible. That way you don't have to worry about scammers or unethical third-parties trying to cheat you. It's your safest, surest line of contact.

Recruiters

Think of recruiters as matchmakers. They have a sweet little open job and they'd love to find a dev who's a perfect fit for it. While devs at smaller studios or indies do recruitment on top of their regular duties, larger studios have staff whose sole responsibility is finding the right candidate for each role. Keep your LinkedIn profile up to date and flip on the "I'm looking" switch so you'll show up in recruitment searches.

Staffing Agencies

I hear new writers complain that the games industry doesn't hire juniors any-more, but that's not true. Junior roles are often outsourced contract gigs now, filled by freelancers or large staffing agencies. These agencies take a big chunk of your salary, and offer limited benefits and career development, but they *do* help you gain critical experience. Contractors sometimes "get converted" to fulltime, in-house devs after they've proven themselves on the job. It's not the norm, but it happens. If you decide to go this route, read up on the dark side of contract work[2] first. Or skip the big staffing firms entirely and try "merc work"[3] at a friendly smaller agency like Sweet Baby Inc or Talespinners instead.

HOW DO I KNOW IT'S A GOOD PLACE TO WORK?

You've seen headlines about toxic, bullying, crunch-tastic places to work in games. How can you sort the good guys from the bad guys? Honestly, there's no way to be sure. Every place has its own issues and quirks that may or may not align with your personal values. But there are some signals that a studio's culture might be a problem. Take these steps:

- Check Glassdoor.com to see what people say about the studio's practices.
- Follow people from that studio on social media. Not just the high-profile "names," but people doing the job you want. How do they talk about their day to day? Are they always tired and drained? Do you see them posting about work on weekends or after hours? Do they all seem to have financial woes? These are signs that you should look deeper into their culture.
- Look at the verbiage on company websites and job posts. Language is a big tell. Gendered sentences like "Our ideal candidate knows what he wants" are revealing. Most companies screen for gendered language and imagery on their websites these days, so beware a place that doesn't. You want to see collaborative, inclusive language that signals you'll be welcome there.
- Speaking of values, watch out for any place that valorizes crunch. "Our ideal candidate makes the most of their 25-hour day." Yeah. You know what you're in for there.
- Some studios have a "frat party" mentality left over from the early days of video games. If the company spends more time touting their beer fridge and ball pit than they do their flexible schedules and generous PTO, it says something about what their culture values.

- Are you having trouble figuring out what the job is? That's not a good sign. Vague language means the studio doesn't know or doesn't want to say. Either way, you'll end up performing a role (or several!) that aren't what you signed up for. This isn't a deal-breaker, but make sure you pin down what the role is and does before taking it.

IS THIS JOB RIGHT FOR ME?

Only you can answer that question, but if the role sounds interesting, there are some encouraging signs that suggest you'd be happy there. Here are some things to look for:

- Salary information – Upfront statements of salary bands show a refreshing straightforwardness. (It's now required by law in some regions. Heck yeah!)
- Clear statement of benefits or unusual benefits, such as a health stipend or child care.
- If you need to move for the role, look for mention of a relocation plan.
- Marginalized folks should look for neutral language in the job post and on the studio website.

With all this in mind, which place would you rather work for?

| Studio A | "We're looking for a rockstar developer who lives, breathes, eats, and sweats his job. He chugs a Monster for breakfast and isn't afraid to burn the midnight oil. If you want to be the best in the business, there's a place for you at Studio A. Join us!" |
| Studio B | "Our ideal candidate is a skilled creative who knows how to make their work shine in a team of industry luminaries. We offer competitive salaries and benefits, generous PTO, and a fun, collaborative atmosphere." |

It's purely a matter of individual taste, but I run screaming from ads like Studio A's. Read the ad carefully to decide if it's the right role and right studio for you. If it is, get ready to embark on the wild ride of applying for game-writing jobs.

NOTES

1   "JD's Game Jobs List." Jan David Hassel. Last accessed April 30, 2023. https://docs.google.com/document/d/1CU1H-8ZQWUPIBrT3VaUjjSMpOrarfpfhI86q8Bkpr_8/edit
2   Campbell, Colin. Polygon. Dec 19, 2016. https://www.polygon.com/features/2016/12/19/13878484/game-industry-worker-misclassification
3   Mercenary work, that is, sword for hire. Doing one-off contract gigs for an agency.

Introduce Yourself

4

So, you've found a job that interests you and you're ready to go for it. It's the perfect job for you! You *crave* this job! Okay, okay! Simmer down. Before you hurl your resume at the studio, ask yourself this: Am I the right person for this role?

AM I QUALIFIED FOR THIS JOB?

The role description seems like a good fit, but then you see the requirements. The skill list is daunting, and what's all this about shipped games? Before you panic, here's a quick way to tell if it's the right role for you: title, education, experience, and skill.

Title

Check my experience table (Table 4.1) to see if you're at the right level for the role. But don't automatically walk away if you're not! Especially you marginalized folks. People frequently apply for roles in the tier above theirs, so it's worth a shot. But if you apply 2–3 tiers above your experience level, then you're rolling the dice, my friend. You *might* land the gig, but be realistic about your chances. Someone with one year of games experience is unlikely to get handed the keys to a AAA project as a director. Your odds are best within your tier or one level above.

The experience ranges are rough estimates, not a hard industry rule. There are many, many exceptions. Like me! I've been making games for almost two decades and choose to stay a lead. I know senior-level freelancers with thirty years' experience. And I've seen folks brought in to write screenplays with no games experience at all. It all depends on the studio, the project, and *you*.

DOI: 10.1201/9781003282259-5

TABLE 4.1   Estimated job experience by tier and title

TIER	TITLE (TITLE PREFIX INDICATED WITH *)	EXPERIENCE IN YEARS
Junior	• Intern • Junior * • Associate *	0–2
Mid-level	• Writer/Scriptwriter/Screenwriter • Narrative Designer • Intermediate *	2–4
Senior	• Advanced * • Senior * • Principal * or Expert *	3–5
Leadership	• Associate Lead * • Lead * or * Manager • Associate Director * • Director *	5+

Education

Unless there's an academic element to the role or you're planning to move abroad, ignore the education requirement. I'm dead serious. Don't worry about it. Hands-on experience matters more.

Experience

Experience isn't just years, it's mileage. If you've been in games for three years, what have you learned? That "must have shipped two games" requirement is designed to weed out people who don't understand the pipelines and processes of taking a game through a full development cycle. If you understand the realities of development or have comparable experience, then you're fine. Same goes for specific types of experience. Consider "familiarity with branching dialogue" or "experience with a writing room process" nice-to-haves.

Here's a tip: If you're making the leap from small indie titles to AAA roles, mid-level is the sweet spot for that leap—with a one-level experience disparity. For example, a senior indie writer can land a mid-level AAA job, but probably not the reverse. There are exceptions, of course, but this is the unspoken rule.

Skill

This part is simple. Can you do the job? Worry less about the specific software the ad lists and focus instead on the underlying skills of your craft. That's the stuff they can't teach. So, if the ad calls for "familiarity with Final Draft," you're golden if you can write a solid screenplay. Also, don't worry about ticking every box. If you have roughly half or more of the skills, go for it.

HOW DO I READ THIS JOB POST?

Let's look at this Textbox Studios ad for a writer (Figure 4.1).[1] Read through the ad carefully, look for the points we just discussed, and see if any keywords jump out at you.

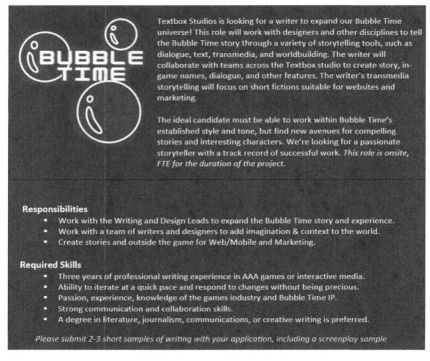

Textbox Studios is looking for a writer to expand our Bubble Time universe! This role will work with designers and other disciplines to tell the Bubble Time story through a variety of storytelling tools, such as dialogue, text, transmedia, and worldbuilding. The writer will collaborate with teams across the Textbox studio to create story, in-game names, dialogue, and other features. The writer's transmedia storytelling will focus on short fictions suitable for websites and marketing.

The ideal candidate must be able to work within Bubble Time's established style and tone, but find new avenues for compelling stories and interesting characters. We're looking for a passionate storyteller with a track record of successful work. *This role is onsite, FTE for the duration of the project.*

Responsibilities
- Work with the Writing and Design Leads to expand the Bubble Time story and experience.
- Work with a team of writers and designers to add imagination & context to the world.
- Create stories and outside the game for Web/Mobile and Marketing.

Required Skills
- Three years of professional writing experience in AAA games or interactive media.
- Ability to iterate at a quick pace and respond to changes without being precious.
- Passion, experience, knowledge of the games industry and Bubble Time IP.
- Strong communication and collaboration skills.
- A degree in literature, journalism, communications, or creative writing is preferred.

Please submit 2-3 short samples of writing with your application, including a screenplay sample

FIGURE 4.1   An example job post.

I know this job post looks intimidating at first glance, but it's pretty simple:

- **Title**: There's no modifier on the title (such as junior or lead), so you know this is a mid-level role.
- **Education**: A college degree is "preferred" not required, so ignore it.
- **Skills**: Can you write well in their house style? Are you familiar with the various working parts of a video game? Are you creative? Can you write short fiction pieces and marketing material? Can you handle feedback? Then, you're qualified!
- **Experience**: They emphasize experience in a few places, so expect to be on the higher end of a mid-level's 2–4 years.

Keywords:

- You'll find the Three Cs (Communication, Collaboration, Craft) in almost every job post. These are core skills.
- Variations of "don't be precious" appear in most job ads. Giving and receiving feedback is part of game writing's iterative process. It's a must-have.
- "Work with others" means being a team player. It's putting the needs of the project above your own darlings—even when it hurts.
- Jot down any specifics the ad calls out: transmedia, worldbuilding, marketing, web/mobile, dialogue, text, imagination, and the IP (in this case, Bubble Time). If it calls out specific programs like Perforce or Final Draft, note those for later.

Pretty simple, right? The ad sets a baseline level of skill, but still leaves room for different areas of expertise. That's its purpose. Just remember that all requirements are negotiable if you can write what the studio needs. Talent and skill trump everything.

HOW DO I APPLY FOR A JOB?

Online applications are self-explanatory these days. Most major studios have fillable forms that cover the essential information, and your attached resume fills in the blanks. Sometimes you fill in the application blanks *and* send your resume with the same info. (Shout-out to everyone who's had to do that. If you know, you know.) Have the standard application materials of resume, cover letter, and writing samples ready before you apply, as some applications will time out if you take too long. If you apply through a service like Taleo or Jobvite, make sure to save your account information for other applications.

WHAT DO RECRUITERS LOOK FOR?

Recruiters are your primary audience. Only a small percentage of applications get sent on to hiring managers, so you have to impress the recruiter first. Convince them you're perfect for this job—and hurry! Recruiters have a "30-second rule." That's how long they spend looking at the average application. That's how long you have to tick all the boxes.

> **Note**: Applicants complain that recruiters or companies "don't know what they want" when they're hiring. I know it seems that way, but you never know what's happening behind the scenes. Maybe requirements shift because the project bloated or features got cut. Perhaps internal priorities changed. Flux means that previously "perfect" candidates no longer match the project needs. It's tough on everybody when it happens, but it's not malicious.

WHEN'S THE BEST TIME TO APPLY FOR JOBS?

The "best" time varies by project, but there are some universal bad times. Fresh graduates flood the market with resumes in April and May, so your app might get lost in the crowd. Some studios close for the winter holidays (Christmas, Hanukkah, New Year, etc.) so your application could languish for weeks. European studios close shop in July for summer vacation. Go ahead and apply during those windows, but be patient if the application process moves slower.

WHEN SHOULD I NUDGE THE STUDIO?

You applied, a recruiter wrote back, everything was going great—then they ghosted you. What do you do? First, don't assume it's deliberate. Some studios receive over a thousand applications *every day* for a single writing role, so it's easy for one to slip through the cracks. Or maybe the project needs changed and the recruiter is waiting for an update before getting back to you. Whatever the reason, stay professional and follow these guidelines.

- Application with no response: If you sent in an application and never heard back, move on. You can wait a few weeks and send a "Hey, did you receive my application?" nudge, but your best tactic is to fire and forget. Some studios don't send rejection notices for the first-round "slush pile" of applications. There are too many.
- Application with response: If a recruiter contacted you about your application and then disappeared, ping them. Wait *no less than* one week and *usually about* two, then email to politely nudge them. Wait another week, then nudge them again. If you hear nothing after two reminders, let it go. It feels bad, I know, but you don't have a choice. Move on!
- In the hiring process: If you get ghosted once you're a round or two into the hiring process and have established a solid dialogue, definitely ping the studio with reminders. Especially if they said they'd get back to you by a certain date. Stay polite and friendly, but the normal rules of correspondence apply here.

SHOULD I REAPPLY FOR A JOB?

What if the studio says "no" for one job, but then they post a new job that's a better fit? Should you apply? Yes! If you were rejected for a senior role and they post a mid-level job, go for it! But *don't do the reverse*. Unless the studio specifically said, "Wow, you're way overqualified for this mid-level gig! You should apply for the senior role," you won't get hired for a more senior role than the one you were rejected for.

If months pass and you notice the company is still hiring for the job you didn't get, ping the recruiter and see what's up. Maybe they haven't found the right person yet? There's no harm in asking. You can also reapply for the *same* role if your skills or experience have improved to align you more closely with the requirements. But otherwise, recruiters recommend waiting six months to a year before applying for the same role again.

WHAT IF THE ANSWER IS NO?

Welcome to Club Rejection! You're in good company. Every professional writer joins us here, sooner or later. Rejection is a normal part of our lives. It's hard to believe, but you'll get used to it. Get feedback early in your career, so you can learn to roll with negative responses. Look for patterns in your rejections. Note what gets successful results and what doesn't. Refine and improve your submission materials. Above all, remember that rejections aren't personal. Only one writer can get that job you applied for. One writer out of thousands. It wasn't you this time. So what? It doesn't make you a bad writer or a bad person. A million factors outside your control can lead to a no. Don't take it to heart. Keep looking. All it takes is one yes, and you're on your way.

SHOULD I ASK FOR FEEDBACK?

Yes. Always. That's how you improve. There's no guarantee you'll get any, but it doesn't hurt to ask.

WHAT IF THEY WON'T GIVE ME FEEDBACK?

There are countless explanations for why a studio might not provide feedback. You can't know what they are, so shrug and move on. I've noticed a growing sense of entitlement to studio feedback recently, and it disturbs me. So here are some reasons why you might not get feedback:

- Good, insightful, constructive feedback takes time to write. Even the best-intentioned studio can't give feedback to thousands of candidates per role. It's impossible.
- Some candidates don't respond well to feedback. They argue and get nasty about it. Of course, *you* would never, but it happens. More often than it should.

- Your work wasn't seen by someone qualified to assess it. Recruiters give feedback on your application, but hiring managers usually give critiques for writing samples. If your application is rejected by the recruiter, the manager never sees your samples.
- Finally, nobody *owes* you feedback. It's not the studio's job to help you improve as a writer, just because you applied. Many studios offer feedback anyway, out of courtesy. The further you get in the hiring process, the more you can reasonably expect critique of your work. If you take a writing test, for example, you should get feedback with your rejection.

DO I NEED TO WRITE A COVER LETTER?

The Short Answer

Nope! There. You're free! Go play some video games. I see your skeptical look, but really. If you don't want to write a cover letter, don't.

The Long Answer

It's complicated. Personally, I find that most cover letters don't do what they should and almost never affect your chances one way or the other. I've hired candidates who didn't submit one, so it's completely optional. But cover letters are a boon to writers. More than any other discipline, we get to show off our craft in the application materials. It's like a built-in audition! Smart candidates recognize this and use it as an opportunity to sell themselves. So, yes. Write one if you're given the chance. Seize every opening the company gives you to explain what you bring to the table.

WHAT MAKES A GOOD COVER LETTER?

Hiring managers read some awful cover letters. They're boring, cliched, and repetitive, or cringy, try-hard, and loooong. It's hard to please both recruiters and hiring managers, especially when accounting for individual tastes. But those constraints mean that candidates end up with dull, corporate-sounding letters or go wildly off brief to show off. The best game-writing cover letters land somewhere in the middle.

HOW DO I WRITE A GOOD COVER LETTER?

I won't give you a template because that cookie-cutter feeling is exactly what you want to avoid. But I'll walk you through the process, step by step.

- Address the studio, not a specific person. Many people will read your letter, from recruiters to (hopefully!) narrative directors. Addressing the studio covers all these possible readers and doesn't lead to awkward situations where you're reading a letter addressed to your colleagues. Try greetings like "Dear Epic Games" or "Hi Failbetter!"
- Before writing, list the important beats of your letter. This is all the critical info that your resume can't or doesn't cover.
  - Who you are.
  - What interests you about the studio or game.
  - A brief summary of your resume ("a game dev with three years of experience making RPGs" is a solid summary.) But brief means a sentence or two, tops.
  - Most important of all, answer this question: Why should the studio hire *you* over all the other applicants?
- Assemble these beats the same way you would a readable in a video game: a hook in the intro lines, the meat of the critical info, and then a satisfying conclusion.
- Write the letter in a conversational tone. This is where so many people go wrong! "Treat it like a writing sample" doesn't mean you should write a short story. Make your writing sound like a person, not a corporate newsletter. Ideally, it should sound like *you*. Avoid all that stiff, formal, corporate language and write the way you speak. Make it interesting. You don't have to be witty or jokey or on-tone for the game, but your job as a writer is to entertain. If you can't hold someone's interest for a few paragraphs, it's not an auspicious sign for your work in the game.

- Keep it short. Two or three brief paragraphs at most. Again, this is a chance to show that you can write the punchy, economical writing that games need.
- Make sure you include your contact info and a link to your portfolio. Here's where you can call out which samples the studio should look at. Don't be afraid to guide them to your best and most appropriate material. "My portfolio can be found at AnnasWork.com. My *Dishonored* samples might interest you."

Keep it short, straightforward, and stimulating. Save the letter as a pdf with this filename format: [FirstnameLastname_CoverLetter]. Keep the.doc version so you can personalize it for each application. And voila! Done.

Extra Credit

Here are some extra tips that will help you get noticed:

- Sincerity goes a long way. A little flattery ("I loved your last game!") is expected, but blatantly untrue fawning is icky.
- If the company makes your favorite game, tell them! Familiarity with the series lore and characters gives you a huge advantage over non-players. Always include that information in your letter.
- Explain resume issues. Say there's a two-year gap in your employment history. Here's where you tell the studio how productively you spent that time. Candidates often try to cover up work from outside the games industry, but that's not necessary. Just outline how it's relevant in your cover letter. You were a kids' camp counselor? Describe how it gave you better organizational skills, taught you modern tween slang, or makes you ideally suited for kids' games.
- But don't clutter up your letter with unrelated "fun facts." Everything should directly relate to the job you're applying for.

WHAT SHOULD A COVER LETTER *NOT* SAY?

Time for the lightning round!

- Don't just regurgitate what's on your resume. New information only, please.

- Don't be flip or sarcastic. Those tones never land the way you think they will. They usually come across as rude or grating. Casual is great; flip is not.
- Don't get overly familiar. You might know the hiring manager from social media (or think you know them) but many people besides them will see this letter. Stay professional.
- Don't namedrop unless you want the studio to contact that "name" about you.
- Don't ramble on for three pages. Keep it succinct and punchy.

P.S. RELAX

Don't stress about your cover letter too much. They rarely make or break an application. At worst, they're a lost opportunity. At best, you've introduced yourself and made the studio curious to know more. Neither reaction will win or lose the job, so write a nice conversational note that explains why they should hire you and pour effort into your resume and samples.

NOTE

1   I assembled this ad from lines pulled from real-life job posts.

Resume
Speaking

5

WHAT MAKES A GOOD RESUME?

You have thirty seconds to convince a recruiter you're right for the job. *Thirty seconds.* Your resume must show, at a glance, that your skill set translates to the specific role you want. If not, it goes in the bin. So how do you do it? How do you write a resume that passes the test and gets you to the next step of the hiring process? Let's start with the basics.

WHAT SHOULD A RESUME INCLUDE?

Here's the baseline information you should put in your resume:

- Your name (Seriously.)
- Contact information (Important!)
- Relevant job history
- Relevant skills *and their context*
- Education, certification, or professional membership *if relevant*
- A link to your website if you have one
- A link to your online portfolio if you have one

Break that information into bullet-pointed sections and keep it under one page. That's it! Simple, right? Yet so many resumes fail these basic criteria on every level. They're hard to read or skimpy or fluffed with unnecessary information. So let's walk through making a *good* resume step by step.

DOI: 10.1201/9781003282259-6

WHERE DO I FIND A GOOD RESUME TEMPLATE?

Pick a resume template from any online site such as Canva and Google docs. Why pay when excellent free choices exist? Just don't go wild with the template. A pop of color in the header is great, but beware of resumes with colors or patterns that make them hard to read. And make sure the font is a reasonable size. The standard is a 12-point font for legibility.

WHAT'S THE BEST RESUME FORMAT?

Here's where things get dicey. How do you arrange all the interesting facts about your skills and experience to highlight your strengths? If you're an experienced pro, the standard chronological (or reverse chronological) works best. Slap that current prestigious job at the top and then list your work history below it. This format showcases your career progression. If your current role is senior writer, and you were a writer and junior writer before that, then recruiters can see how you worked your way up to your current role. I call this resume format The Classic because it's been a serviceable standard for decades. The layout looks something like Resume Genius's "Chicago" Format. All the basics laid out in reverse chronological order by date and role.

But what if you're just starting out? Is there a way to highlight your skills rather than your lack of experience? Yes, there is! A skill-based resume focuses on what you know how to do, not what you've done. *However*, this can be dangerous. There's an alarming trend these days toward "deconstructed resumes." The idea behind them—focusing on skills, not experience—is smart, but the execution is, well…awful. The deconstructed resume gets its name because it detaches skills from the context of experience. Skills float by themselves under one heading and relevant experience is detached from it in another section. Something like this:

SKILLS	*WORK EXPERIENCE*
• Finished work to deadline	• Barista 2017–2019
• Leadership	• Server 2019–2020
• Multitasking	• Content Writer 2021–Present

If I'm a hiring manager (and I often am!), this resume becomes a puzzle for me. I find myself trying to connect the skill in column A with the context in column B. Where did you learn leadership skills? Was it in your job as a barista or your role as content writer? I have no way to know, and it matters. This style of resume looks like you're trying to conceal that information. "I'm hiding something" is not a great impression to make. Here's what I mean. What's more convincing to you?

VERSION A	VERSION B
• Management	Lead Barista
• Team player	• Managed a team of seven
• Goal-oriented	• Exceeded sales targets year over year
• Award-winning	• Awarded "Best Shop" three times

Both options give you roughly the same information. But A is a list of empty buzzwords, while B doesn't just list the skills, it contextualizes them. Sure, the experience isn't in games, but at least I see where you got it. I don't have to just take your word for those skills; you're demonstrating with specific examples that you can lead a team and get excellent results. That's a valuable, transferrable skill. You can see how context makes all the difference and helps you sell yourself. That's what gets lost with deconstructed resumes. If that's not convincing enough, I'll add that I spoke with dozens of recruiters and hiring managers for my *Guide*, and they universally dislike the format. Don't say you weren't warned!

But let's say you heed the warning. You don't want to use the boring old Classic and the Deconstructed has a bad rep, so what should you do? Try a hybrid (Figure 5.1).

This resume has all the important elements, plus a short summary at the top to really sell yourself to the recruiter in that 30-second window. Attaching skills to roles helps contextualize your experience and gives you an opportunity to explain how your experience applies to games.

Content

When you're first breaking into games, you won't have much (or any) industry experience. That's fine! No, really. There's nothing wrong with listing

NONA MAGLEY

Tiny Town, Norway | Nona.Magley@NM.com| NonaMagley.com

GAME WRITER

An experienced game writer with a passion for storytelling. I can write in a range of styles and tones have a "communication and collaboration first" approach to my work. I'm familiar with a range of interactive media programs, including Twine and Trello. I'm a huge Bubble Time fan!

WORK EXPERIENCE

Writer | Indie Darling Games
Oct 2020 - present

- Write text and dialogue according to house style for award-winning independent titles.
- Collaborate with designers and other disciplines to realize the game narrative.

Writer | Cats Are Awesome! Website
Jan 2019 - Sept 2020

- Wrote interactive stories for popular cat-themed website
- Collaborated with Design and Marketing on weekly releases of cat-related content
- Coordinate the release of timed "events" with local media outlets

Blogger | Global Adventures
May 2017 - August 2018

- Created articles and "adventure stories" for travel-themed website
- Met deadlines in high-pressure situations around the world
- Wrote guides and reviews to high standard for marketing purposes

SKILLS

- Able to write in "house style"
- Interactive writing and narrative design
- Excellent communicator

- Team player
- Creative
- Thrives under pressure

EDUCATION
Sept 2014 - May 2017

Local College | College Town

- Studied Process planning, coordination, and efficiency

FIGURE 5.1   An ideal resume.

non-games work. Just make sure you show *how your skills translate to games.* Especially if it's not something obvious. If someone is making the leap from writing for television to games, then I know they're bringing a certain skill set with them. But if you're breaking in from, say, retail sales, then it's up to you to explain how your skills apply to games. For example, does it matter that you make a good cappuccino? Er… It might for some games, but generally you should try to find the universal skills from your previous jobs. Take that list of keywords from the last chapter and find ways that your previous roles used them (Table 5.1).

TABLE 5.1   Transferable skills from non-industry roles

JOB	EXPERIENCE	TRANSFERABLE SKILLS
Barista	Made drinks at busy cafe with coworkers. Took customer orders at register and made customized beverages for them.	Collaboration, fast-paced work to deadlines, good communication, tracking tasks, adaptability, fulfilling a brief, etc.
Retail Sales	Managed a team of three at a local shoe store. Met frequent sales targets. Won Shop of the Month for high sales three years running.	Management, leadership, marketing, communication, successful pitching, team player, goal-oriented, etc.

Take those transferable skills and list them *with context* so it's clear how they were applied, and you've made that experience relevant. Here's how that barista entry might look:

- Barista, The Java Joint (2019–2021): Collaborated with a large team in a fast-paced work environment. Good communication was essential to fill customer briefs to their specifications.

Now you've made your experience relevant, and the hiring manager understands what you mean by "good communication" skills.

WHAT ARE THE DOS AND DON'TS OF RESUMES?

Do

Include any part of your work history or personal experience that applies to games. Any games-related training, awards, studies, etc. that you think directly apply to game writing and to the specific role you're applying for. List your degrees and certifications but don't linger on them. One bullet point for the degree and institution is fine. List hobbies only if they're relevant. I mean, if you're applying to write for a roller derby social sim then you should *absolutely* say that you rollerblade in your spare time.

Don't

Never include experiences or activities that are unrelated to the role. Fantastic that you watch your kid's little league games every Friday, but unless that's somehow relevant to the job (and it might be! *Blaseball*, anyone?) why mention it? List courses of study that directly relate to game writing or design, but think twice before mentioning unrelated training. For example, why mention gourmet cooking classes when applying for a shooter? And don't list your GPA.[1] I promise you, nobody cares.

Especially Don't

When you're first starting out, your resume will feel skimpy, so you'll feel the irresistible urge to fluff it. Be careful when you do this. It's natural and good to present your work in the best light and to find the selling point of all your accomplishments. You should do that! But there's a difference between being the primary writer for a game and writing, say, a few barks or item descriptions. Don't take credit for work you didn't do. Especially don't take credit for other people's work. This is a tiny industry and you'll get found out eventually.

Your application often requires you to sign a statement that the information contained within it is true to the best of your knowledge. That statement gives companies grounds to dismiss you later if it turns out you've misrepresented your education or credentials. And yes, people get fired for lying on their resumes and applications. It happens, so don't do it. It's not worth it.

DO I NEED A RESUME SERVICE OR CAREER COACH?

Y'all, there are some predatory advisors and services out there. Beware of any place that offers "one-size-fits-all" templates for resumes. Beware of resume services that push the "deconstructed" format to hide inexperience. And especially beware any service that has an "anything goes if it gets you an interview" philosophy. If you get an interview by lying on your resume, you'll probably get found out. I've had many interviews where the candidate was obviously trying to bluff their way through. It's not a good look. Be honest and emphasize what you *do* know.

All this to say that you don't need a resume service. Pick a solid, clear resume template and fill it in yourself with the baseline information from my checklist above. Find ways to connect your experience to valuable game-writing skills and highlight those strengths. We tend to downplay our own accomplishments, so have a close friend look it over. Are you selling yourself short? Are you forgetting important skills? Are you far more fabulous than your resume says? They'll remind you. That personal touch is better than a service. If you want more eyeballs on it, post it in The DIN's workshopping chat, in Work with Indies, or any similar writing community.

WHAT'S A KEYWORD PASS?

Once you're satisfied with your resume's content, go back through and do a keyword pass. Take your list of keywords from the ad in Chapter 3 and weave them into your resume. But don't just toss them in as empty buzzwords! Candidates focus on getting past resume-scanning software and forget that living, breathing people will read the resume too. Imagine clapping your human eyes on this statement: "I'm a good communicator who enjoys interactive narrative and collaboration in a team environment." Awful, isn't it? Congrats on cramming a bunch of keywords into one sentence, I guess, but what is it really saying? It's generic. Just like storytelling, the right details in resume text can make it sing. "I collaborated with a design team to craft an interactive story about growing up in Bali. We were able to communicate the history of the region through songs and picture puzzles." You're using the same keywords, but your personality and interests are shining through. I'm going to ask you about that game during our interview, I promise you.

HOW DO I FILE MY RESUME?

Once you've done your keyword pass, have someone check it for typos (you can never see your own) and save it in two formats: doc and pdf. Name the file in this format:

- FirstnameLastname_StudionameResume.

I sometimes add the year for my own tracking purposes.

- AnnaMegill_TextboxStudiosResume2023

It's important you put your name in the file name! Some candidates forget and send stuff like "MyBestResume2022" or "awesomegamewritingresume." Eek.

Keep a doc version of the file so you can easily tailor it to each job you apply for, but only send pdfs with applications. I usually update LinkedIn to match my current resume, but that's entirely optional.

And that's it! That's how you write a killer resume. If you put all this advice together, here's the basic flow.

HOW DO I WRITE A RESUME STEP BY STEP?

- Step 1: Gather all your job history info.
- Step 2: Pick a resume format that highlights your strengths.
- Step 3: Pull out keywords from the job post. Collaboration, communication, nonlinear narrative—whatever the job post called out as important, make sure you include it in your resume. Show that you have the right skills and experience for *this particular* job.
- Step 4: Fill out the template, making sure to include those keywords. Writers tend to get text-y on their resumes, so keep it concise.
- Step 5: Put a summary at the top of your resume for the recruiter's 30-second scan. It should be 4–6 sentences that sum up the details of your resume. The summary should focus on facts and skills and be chock full of those keywords from the job post.
- Step 6: Save and name your files.

Remember that the purpose of your resume is to show recruiters and hiring managers *what* you've done and *how* you've done it. This is the place for facts and straightforward information. Too many people try to stuff personality into their resume when that's not its purpose. Let the facts persuade people. Your skills—and that includes so-called soft skills like collaboration and communication—should stand on their own merit. Save the personality for your cover letter.

NOTE

1   GPA = grade point average. This is a rookie mistake (I made it!) and it screams inexperience. List your university degree and any special training (editing courses, design classes) but skip the grades.

Showcase
Your Work

6

DO I NEED TO SHOW WRITING SAMPLES?

Writing's our craft, and samples prove we're good at it. So, yes, at some point in the hiring process, you'll be asked to share samples. Few writers are exempt from that standard part of the process. When they are, it's because they have a large body of work and their capabilities and talents are well known. They're usually A Name in our industry, like Rhianna Pratchett or Greg Kasavin. I'm not one of those legendary writers, and you're most likely not either. For us, strong writing samples are the key to getting work.

WHAT SAMPLES SHOULD I SEND?

It's tempting to say a good sample is your best work, but that's not entirely true. A good sample is your strongest work *that fits the project* you're applying to. Your best work might be a glorious high-fantasy adventure novel. But if the game is a gritty shooter, it's not going to sell you to the studio. Read the instructions for samples carefully to make sure you're giving the studio what they want.

Fill the Brief

Most studios will say something like "Send three samples of no more than ten pages, including one screenplay." That's a pretty standard request. My job ad in Chapter 3 asks for it. But what does it mean? I'll dissect it for you.

 DOI: 10.1201/9781003282259-7

- "Three samples." Ideally, this means three *distinct* samples, not three excerpts of the same script.
- "No more than ten pages" means ten pages total, not ten per sample. So don't send your whopping ninety-page screenplay unless they specifically ask for it. When a tome like that lands on my desk, I pick ten pages to read at random and hope for the best. But I might miss your best writing that way. Don't chance it. Control the experience and give studios exactly what you want them to read.
- "Including one screenplay." That's straightforward, right? It doesn't mean you can't include more. You can make all three samples a screenplay if you'd like. I've done it because screenplays are valuable for AAA work. But keep the type of game in mind and include work that shows the studio you can do the range of writing needed, from item descriptions to casting documents. Send a cutscene, a readable, and maybe a character bio or branching conversation. Show your range.
- Try to match the tone of the project. If you did your research and learned that the project is, say, a gritty Western shooter, then send your strongest work in that genre or style. What's that? You don't have any samples that suit the project you're applying for? In that case, you have three options:

1. Send your strongest writing that doesn't match the style or tone of the project.
2. Take an existing sample and adjust it to match the style and tone of the project. (Example: take your high-fantasy work and rewrite it for a science fiction game.)
3. Write something new. This might be your only option if they ask for a screenplay sample and you don't have one. It's extremely risky to submit unpolished work, but a skilled and confident writer can pull it off. If that's you, go for it.

Interactive Work

Increasingly, studios want samples of interactive work, especially for narrative design roles. Twine games, specifically, get a nod in some job ads. If you submit an interactive sample, keep it short. Make sure players can reach your strongest work in under five minutes. If you submit a Twine game that requires 20 minutes of play before you hit the good stuff, no one will see it. If it's all you have, then submit a video version of the game that hiring managers can scrub through. Timestamp the material you want them to look at—and make sure they don't need the 20 minutes of lead-in play for it to make sense. Post it on YouTube, Twitch, or in your portfolio and link it in your cover letter.

The Rules

- Submit your strongest, most polished work that best matches the project's needs.
- If you have an existing sample that fits the brief in tone and style, polish and submit it.
- If you have nothing similar in style and tone, then simply submit your best work.
- If the studio requests a specific type of sample (audio logs for example) submit your best work in that format. If you have nothing in that format, either rework an existing sample or submit your strongest work in a different format.

The goal of samples is to demonstrate that you can write what the studio needs. But don't Kermit-flail if you can't perfectly match the project tone. You'll have a second chance to write in the house style with their writing test.

Contextualize!

Give your samples some context: If you've plucked your sample from a larger work, like one scene from a long mission, explain how it fits into the flow. Some writers provide long character bios and pages of story synopsis to frame the scene. That's too much. The backstory is practically its own sample! Provide just enough context for readers to understand the scene.

Look at the two examples of dramatic scenes in Tables 6.1 and 6.2.

You can see what a big difference a little context makes. It helps readers can understand the subtext of Millie's "What's wrong with you?" line.

TABLE 6.1   A dramatic scene without context

A VISITOR
Kenan: Hey, Mill! You okay? Here. I brought some flowers to liven things up around here.
Millie: What's wrong with you?
Kenan: I…oh. Sorry. Wasn't thinking.

TABLE 6.2   A dramatic scene with context

A VISITOR

It's the anniversary of her daughter Lily's death, and Millie is grieving at home when she gets an unexpected visit from Kenan. He's brought a bouquet of lilies as a gift.

Kenan: Hey, Mill! You okay? Here. I brought some flowers to liven things up around here.

Millie: What's wrong with you?

Kenan: I…oh. Sorry. Wasn't thinking.

WHAT SHOULD I *NOT* SEND AS SAMPLES?

- Don't send unpolished work. Never send work that hasn't had other eyes on it.
- Romance and erotica have their place in games, so don't be afraid to send those samples if they're appropriate for the project. Think hard before sending straight-up pornography, though. Imagine the hiring manager reading it on the fly between meetings in the harsh glare of office lights. Is it going to go over well in those conditions? Probably not.
- Plagiarized work. I once had someone submit *my own writing* to me as a sample. Don't do that. Don't steal other writers' work. Don't claim you wrote something you didn't. Don't try to pass another writer's work off as your own. Don't submit samples that you didn't write. It's shockingly dishonest. You won't get the job, but you will get a bad reputation. It's not worth it.
- Bad attitude. All a studio knows of you is what's on the page. If all your samples are angry or super edgy or filled with pointless profanity, then those choices say something about you as a writer and a person. That bad impression might not be *you*, but we don't know that. Have friends check your work to see what impression you give off.

HOW DO I SUBMIT SAMPLES?

Once you know what you're sending, prepare the samples to send. You have two choices here:

- Update your online portfolio to make sure it's ready for scrutiny.
- Collate the samples into a single packet and attach it to your application.

I've seen both, and either way is fine. If you go with the packet, include a title page or a list of what's in the packet and make sure each sample is clearly marked and defined. Put your name and contact info somewhere *inside* the packet and save the file as [FirstnameLastname]_Samples. For me, the file would read AnnaMegill_Samples. Or if you're applying to several places and have different sample packets, add the studio name too. Example: AnnaMegill_ TextboxStudios_Samples. Attach the packet to the application or email, bid it bon voyage, and you're all set.

HOW DO I MAKE AN INTERACTIVE PORTFOLIO?

It makes me sad to pop open someone's digital portfolio and discover a mess inside. I often see folders and random pages akimbo, with titles like "Screenplay Summer 2021" and "Humor Project 4 Me." It makes my head spin with questions. What's the deal here? What am I supposed to read? Is this how you'll handle files on the project? The story you're telling me isn't good. It's a shame because here's the thing: it's *your* story. Your portfolio is the narrative of you as a writer. When I'm done reading it, I should understand what skills and experience you bring, how you approach writing, and how you think about projects. All of that from a portfolio? You bet. I'll walk you through what I mean.

What's Your Story?

First, decide what story you want your portfolio to tell. After 20 years in the industry, my portfolio tells the story of a seasoned veteran with a large body of work, especially in big-budget cinematic games. I have a bit of every kind of writing in there, with a focus on screenplays and weird stuff. That tells studios what they'll get when they hire me. If you're just starting out and don't have a large body of work yet, you'll tell a different story. Maybe it's the story of raw talent, with a few dazzling samples that show off your skills. Maybe it's your thought process as you walk readers through an entire game, barks and all. You decide what story to convey.

Let's tour my portfolio. I'll show you what I did and suggest ways you can make it your own.

WHAT GOES IN MY PUBLIC PORTFOLIO?

First, some sort of public portfolio is a must. Professional writers need a place to show off their work, especially their interactive work, so studios can find you and hire you. As soon as you can, pull together a website where studios can learn all about you. Wix, WordPress, Squarespace, whatever fits your budget and lets you have a professional online presence, go for it.

Just like your cover letter, your portfolio is an opportunity to express yourself as a writer and let people see what you can do. I find it helpful to have two portfolios: one public, one private. My public portfolio (annamegill.com/games) is a simple grid of images from past projects. If you came to my website with no idea who I was, you could learn my history at a glance. It's a visual resume of my work. The thumbnails link out to the official sites for the game, so you can dive deeper into each project. Students with no published work could link to writing excerpts here instead. Put a thumbnail image that aligns with your project (grab fair-use images from sites like Pexels or Getty Images) and link to short writing excerpts.

WARNING!

Don't post entire samples on public sites. Plagiarism is a growing problem for game writers. If you opt for a public portfolio, only post snippets of your work. Between unethical writers and AI programs gobbling up material, it's best to lock full samples behind a password. But remember to include your password with your application! A fancy portfolio is useless if studios can't access it.

WHAT GOES IN MY PRIVATE PORTFOLIO?

Make your public portfolio flashy and prominent, but keep your private portfolio, well, private. This is the treasure trove! It's where you stash your full samples. It doesn't have to be a fancy dedicated website. Even a plain Dropbox or Google Drive works if you keep it tidy and direct the studio to your relevant work. Use this exclusive space to express yourself and tell your story.

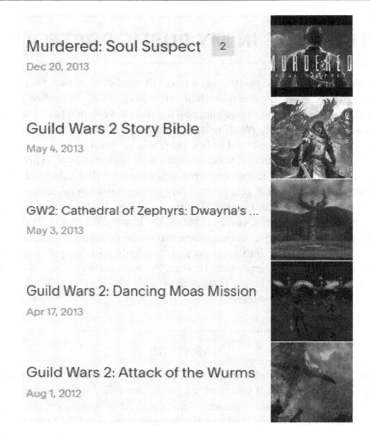

Murdered: Soul Suspect   2
Dec 20, 2013

Guild Wars 2 Story Bible
May 4, 2013

GW2: Cathedral of Zephyrs: Dwayna's ...
May 3, 2013

Guild Wars 2: Dancing Moas Mission
Apr 17, 2013

Guild Wars 2: Attack of the Wurms
Aug 1, 2012

FIGURE 6.1   Private portfolio index.

When you open my private portfolio, there's an index of thumbnails on one side so you can jump easily to the work you want, but the main pages read like a blog. My most recent work is on top, and scrolling through it takes you back in time to my earlier work (Figure 6.1).

I have a blog-style entry for each project, just like the one pictured in Figure 6.2. Each entry has an image, a description of the game, pdfs for online viewing or download, and links to videos of my work in each game, with credit given to colleagues for their contributions. The format is bog standard, so I rely on three factors to make it sparkle: the prestige of the titles, the sheer volume of work available, and, of course, the quality of the work itself. So what story am I telling? My private portfolio continues the story I started on my public page: the story of growing experience and a taste for the strange.

Unreleased Action-Adventure Game

December 15, 2017

Excerpts from an unreleased action-adventure game.

- **Teamed Up - Interactive Cine** [PDF]
- **In the Mines - Mission** [PDF]
- **At the Peak - Cine** [PDF]

FIGURE 6.2   Private portfolio entry.

WHAT DO STUDIOS LOOK FOR IN PORTFOLIOS?

I created a handy-dandy acronym to help you remember what hiring managers look for in portfolios. Keep PROSE in mind as you create your portfolio story.

PROSE

- POLISH: Only include your best, most polished work.
- RANGE: Include a wide variety of work. Dialogue and cinematics, of course, but also barks, objectives, item descriptions, letters, codex entries, and various other bits of text. Include links to some form of interactive writing, too, like a Twine game. Show that you can write everything a game needs.
- ORDER: How you arrange your samples within the portfolio. Always lead with your strongest work. If the studio likes it, they'll read more.

- STYLE: Show that you can write for any type of game. We've covered this!
- EASE: Make your work easy to access. Even if a studio asks for a samples as pdfs, include a link to your full portfolio. Let them know it features Twine games and other interactive media that don't work well as documents.

Of course, studios want to see growth, expertise, talent, and all the other standard tick boxes. But at the end of the day, they have one question: Can you do the job? If your portfolio showcases nothing but barks, they won't know you can handle cinematics or design documentation. If you only have "grimdark" contemporary writing, they'll never know about your light-hearted fantasy romp. Make it easy for them to picture you working on their project. That's what they want.

HOW DO I "TELL MY STORY"?

That's up to you! If you're just starting out, you might focus more on knowledge and potential. Have entries for all the different parts of a game to show you understand them. Walk readers through your process for creating a sample you're especially proud of. Tell the story of your unique writing voice and how you express it through games work. It's your story! Highlight the aspects *you* think are important.

Update the entries as your writing improves and keep adding work until you've covered every part of a project, from item descriptions to cinematics. Not only will you have a portfolio that shows your range, but you'll also have a variety of samples ready to go when you're applying for jobs. If you want to show style, you could have a sample of a "scene written three ways." That means you take the same beats and write them as, say, a comedy, a sci-fi movie, and a horror film. It's entirely up to you! Whatever you decide your story is, lean into that narrative. You're a writer. Storytelling is your strength. You've got this!

In the Spotlight

7

Bwoop! A notification pops on your phone. It's a recruiter, pinging to see when you're free to chat about your application. You got an interview! It's your moment in the spotlight! You're excited at first, then reality strikes: What do you say? How should you act? What do you wear? Don't panic! Interviews aren't film noir interrogations. The studio wants to meet you and answer a simple question: Will you fit into their team?

WHAT IS THE AAA INTERVIEW PROCESS LIKE?

The hiring process is different at every studio. Some companies know you're The One after a single interview, but most AAA studios have a series of screenings and chats that ramp up to an onsite or "panel" interview. Every stage is designed to assess a different aspect of the candidate's knowledge. The flow of these interviews might look like this sketch (Figure 7.1).

The process is shorter at some companies, and some places have those same steps in a different order. Junior roles might skip the full panel interview, but it's a must for seniors. Here's your rule of thumb: the more senior the role, the more rigorous the process. Well-known writers, any "names" on the project, might join the team after a quick gab with leadership, but they're the exception. Most writers trot the full obstacle course on their way to an offer

DOI: 10.1201/9781003282259-8

FIGURE 7.1 The Interview flow.

WHAT CAN I EXPECT AT EACH STEP?

Every studio has its own quirks and expectations for interviews, but most places follow a similar pattern. Here's what I've learned to expect from each of these steps.

The Screen

In AAA, this step is the initial meet-and-greet with a recruiter. They've looked over your resume and application materials, so they think you're a viable candidate. Now, they're making sure your needs align with the studio's. How do you like working with large teams? Can you relocate? What are your salary requirements? When can you start? I jokingly call this interview the "axe-murderer test" because it's a big ol' vibe check. Will you fit into life at that studio, or are you a dangerous sociopath? This is a low-pressure interview (unless you're an actual axe-murderer, I guess), but you should come prepared to talk salary expectations and logistics.

Hiring Manager Interview

If the recruiter gives you the thumbs-up, your next interview is with the hiring manager. They've read your samples, so they might ask about those. They might also ask about your writing process, how you approach storytelling, what lights you up creatively, and what unique skills you bring. This is your craft interview, so come prepared to talk about game narrative, the studio's projects, and the development process. Your goal is to impress the hiring manager with your storytelling knowledge. If you nail this interview, your next step will likely be a writing test.

Follow-Up Interview

If the hiring manager is on the fence about you, there'll be a follow-up interview with them or another senior narrative person. This doesn't mean you "failed" the first interview. They haven't rejected you, so they must recognize your talent. Dazzle them in this interview, and you'll be fine. If this interview comes after the writing test, come prepared to discuss the choices you made on your test.

Team Interview

If you make it to this step, then good news! You're past the hardest part of the process. By now you've probably taken a writing test and convinced the hiring manager that you can do the job. All you need to do now is get along with the team. Have a nice chat with your potential colleagues and get a feel for how you'd all work all together. There's no prep for this round. Be yourself, and enjoy talking shop with other writers!

Studio "Panel" Interview or Onsite

This interview can be tough, mentally and physically. It's a series of get-to-know-you chats with departments like Cinematics, Design, Production, and Audio. They'll ask you the same questions over and over, so relax and give consistent answers. They probably won't discuss storytelling as a craft, but they'll want to know how you see narrative meshing with *their* disciplines. If you make it to this interview, the job is yours to lose. But don't get cocky!

I've seen candidates get rejected at this stage for knocking another team's work or talking over the women in the room. Don't do that. Only a few candidates remain at this stage, so the studio is looking for any reason to distinguish you. Be friendly, polite, and collaborative, and you'll do great.

HOW DO I PREPARE FOR AN INTERVIEW?

I used to stress out over job interviews. I mean real-deal, capital-A anxiety: insomnia the night before, nausea, cold sweats, heart palpitations, vomiting, the works. But as I had more interviews and grew more confident in my abilities, it all got easier. Interviews aren't exams. There aren't right or wrong answers to the questions. The studio simply wants to know how *you* approach storytelling and the game development process. They want to like you! Help them do that, and make them excited about working with you.

Know Your Stuff

Don't go into interviews without doing research. If you can't be bothered to learn basic information about the studio and its games, then yeesh. It's a bad look. I'm not saying you have to memorize the entire 135-year history of Nintendo, but can you at least name some of their games? Also, try to find out who your interviewers are. Research local wages and come prepared to discuss salary expectations. Your goal is to show a studio that you want to work *there* and not any random place that will take you—even if that's the case.

Mock Interviews

Like any skill, interviewing gets better with practice. Have your buddy grill you with questions and practice giving thoughtful, succinct answers. Record yourself, then play back the video to see how you come across. Do you ramble? Freeze up? Forget to answer the question you were asked? Plan ahead for how you'll handle those issues during the interview. I tend to ramble, so when I feel that starting to happen, I circle back to the original question and stop: "So, yeah, that's what makes an interesting character."

SAMPLE INTERVIEW QUESTIONS

Here are some questions you might be asked during interviews:

- Why do you want to work on this game/at this studio?
- Can you walk us through your writing process, from brief to handoff?
- What are some games you think handle narrative well? Or poorly?
- What are your salary expectations?
- How do you think Production (or Mission Design, Concept Art, etc.) fits into the Narrative pipeline?
- What do you think makes an interesting interactive story?
- What do you think of the story in our past games? *(Careful with this one!)*
- What do you hope to get out of this role?

These questions are designed to get you talking about what's important to you, both narratively and in the workplace. Be yourself, answer honestly, and you'll rock it. You might even discover that the role or studio isn't right for you and withdraw from the hiring process. That happens more often than people realize. Don't be afraid to bow out. It's better than ending up in a job you don't like.

WHAT ARE INTERVIEW DOS AND DON'TS?

I'll blaze through these points because they're pure common sense.

Do

- Take a break during long interviews. If you're not offered one, ask for it. Nobody will mind. Studios want you to be comfortable!
- Let the studio know in advance if you need accommodation for a disability. Any good studio will be happy to make necessary adjustments.

- Relax and be yourself. Don't put on an act or be fake. Be on your best behavior, but still be *you*.
- Be kind to yourself if something goes wrong. Life happens! I've watched a cat vomit on the candidate's keyboard during a video interview and seen candidates spill coffee down their shirts. No one's going to hold it against you. Calls drop, connections are bad, errors occur. How you handle the situation matters much more than the incident itself. The best response is to apologize or laugh it off and move on.

Don't

- Don't be overly familiar with your interviewer. Don't flirt, hit them up for a date, or ask personal questions. It's inappropriate for the interview and will likely cost you the job.
- Don't come unprepared. You know they'll ask if you have any questions, so have a few ready. Having no questions makes it seem like you don't care. Curiosity is good.
- Don't be late, reschedule multiple times, or miss the interview without a good reason.
- Don't make your interviewer do all the work. The more like a conversation it is, the more enjoyable it is for everyone. Avoid terse, one-sentence responses.
- Don't show up drunk or high. I've interviewed some stoned candidates before, and it's not fun. For me, anyway.
- Don't be rude, crude, or combative. Yes, I shouldn't have to say it, but here we are.

WHAT'S AN NDA?

At some point during the hiring process, you'll be asked to sign a nondisclosure agreement or NDA. These are legal documents that bind you to secrecy about what you learn during the interview process. In their simplest form, they prevent you from passing along any information or project materials to people outside the studio. Here's some typical NDA language (Figure 7.2).

Dear Nona Magley

You have been invited to Textbox Studios for the purpose of participating in an interview, and possibly a series of interviews, for a position with our company. Textbox develops and publishes interactive entertainment software products. In the course of these interviews it is possible we might share information with you, to learn more about you, your skills and your technical expertise. This information may be confidential and proprietary information of Textbox; it is essential that these discussions be kept confidential. Therefore, before these interviews begin, we ask that you review this letter and sign in the appropriate space, indicating your agreement to the terms and conditions contained herein.

1. Confidential information means all information disclosed by Textbox, or learned by you in the course of your interview(s), that relates to Textbox Studios' or its licensors' technology, intellectual property assets, financial affairs, financial statements, internal management tools and systems, products and product development plans, marketing plans, customers, clients and contracts, and is designated by Textbox as confidential or that a reasonable person would deem to be confidential. ETC.

FIGURE 7.2   Sample NDA text.

SHOULD I SIGN THIS NDA?

Yes. If the NDA sets reasonable restrictions and merely asks you to keep what you see confidential, there's no reason not to sign it. Games are a billion-dollar industry, and their development is smothered in secret sauce. An NDA allows companies to talk freely about projects during an interview without worrying that you'll take that info to their competitors. Take NDAs seriously, but also take advantage of the freedom they give you to learn more about the project. The team is probably excited to discuss what they're working on!

HOW CAN I TELL IF I PASSED THE INTERVIEW?

There are no definite rules! Every studio has its own pass/fail criteria for applicants. Success or failure often comes from unpredictable outside factors as much as the candidates themselves. I try to keep a poker face during interviews because I don't want to give candidates false hope, just in case someone else says no. But that said, here are some encouraging signs:

- The interviewer wants to discuss "next steps."
- The interview runs long. It was supposed to be an hour, but you gabbed for two.
- The interviewer wants to follow up with more information afterward.
- You feel a good rapport.
- They say, "Ha, great joke! You're hired!"

Okay, I'm kidding with that last one, but you get the idea. You can usually tell when an interview has gone well. And the interview you thought was a "total disaster" probably went fine. It's hard to crash and burn, I promise.

WHAT ARE THE "NEXT STEPS"?

After each phase of the interview process, the studio will tell you what the "next steps" are in their process. If they don't tell you, ask. Say, "Thanks for the interview. It was fun talking to you. May I ask what the next step is after this?" Knowing what to expect takes the anxiety out of the process and helps you prepare. Some recruiters will walk you through the entire hiring process if you ask them. The studio decides yes or no after each interview, so each "next step" means you've won a minor battle. Good work, soldier.

Time to Shine

8

WHAT'S A WRITING TEST?

You're cruising through the hiring process! Application? Check. Resume? Check. Interview? Check! Writing test? Ch—what? Ah, we should talk about that. Somewhere in the hiring process for AAA studios, you'll be asked to take a writing test. A test might mean writing a short screenplay or it could mean designing and writing an entire mission, down to the last bark. Some tests are timed, and some have no time limit at all. Every studio whips up its own, unique test. The only predictable part of writing tests is their purpose: assessing your ability to write in the studio's "house style."

WHY DO STUDIOS HAVE WRITING TESTS?

Why, indeed. Aren't samples enough? Can't studios tell you're a good writer from those? Sometimes they can! If you're an established writer with a body of work or if your samples matched the house style, then you might skip the test and move straight to interviews. But otherwise, you'll get the test. The most common reason studios ask for tests is to see if you can write in a specific style or tone. Or maybe your samples reflect a team's work and the studio wants to see your solo work. Or…there's that nasty issue of plagiarism. It's rare, but it happens. Tests can be a boon for new writers who don't have many samples yet. You compete directly with other candidates and show off your skills. Tests also show that you can write outside your comfort zone and follow a brief. For all these reasons, tests will probably be around for a while longer.

DOI: 10.1201/9781003282259-9

SHOULD I TAKE A WRITING TEST?

It's your call! I get why you'd refuse the test. You're working for free! With no guarantee of anything in return. Some longer writing tests take weeks to complete. If you're taking tests for multiple companies, that time adds up fast. Long test times disproportionately impact marginalized communities, who might not have the resources or time to spare. Considering all that, is there any reason why you *would* take a test? Well, I already mentioned one reason: less experienced candidates have a chance to shine. Your samples might not be strong or showcase your talents as well as they could. Tests are an opportunity to show your unique voice and perspective. Remember: a good writing test respects your time. If it's unreasonably long or burdensome, you *should* push back. Propose a shorter test or ask for more time. Most companies are happy to make those accommodations. Talk to the recruiter about your circumstances and see what you can work out. But ultimately, you'll have to decide whether or not to take the test on your own.

WHAT IF I DON'T TAKE THE WRITING TEST?

I'll be honest, it's rare that someone declines the test. Try every other avenue before you turn it down flat. Ask for pay, ask for a shorter test, ask to be accommodated. But if those adjustments don't help or if you asked for reasonable pay and the studio said no, then you'll have to decide if it's worth the trouble. You might decide it's not and move on. Or maybe you hang in there and hope your samples are strong enough to secure the job. They might be! Just be aware that writers who take the test and nail it will have an advantage over you. Declining the test is a gamble, so make that decision with open eyes.

> If you decide to not take a test, then ask if you can submit additional samples that align with their house style or project tone. You'll be assessed by those instead. Alternatively, you can ask to be paid for your time.

CAN I GET PAID FOR THE TEST?

Yes! But ask with your eyes open. Most AAA studios don't pay for testing. That's our current reality. Some candidates ask for pay and get it, while some are flat-out refused. It all depends on you and that company's policies. If you go for it, determine how long you'll need and set a reasonable hourly rate for those hours. The worst that can happen is they'll say no and you'll have to decide if you still want to take the test. It's worth a shot, right?

WHAT DOES A WRITING TEST LOOK LIKE?

My friend, there are some wild tests out there! I've seen tests ask for complete, detailed missions or a pile of supporting documents. Some companies ask for "an entire self-contained Story Mission. The goal is for it to take somewhere between 30-40 minutes to complete and offer a true storytelling experience." One test was multiple tests rolled into one, with a character biography and three examples of character arcs, a screenplay incorporating the character arcs, and a playable Twine game (due in ten days!). But most tests are simple and straightforward. The tests I've created ask you to write a single scene with a few possibilities. Here's an example (Table 8.1).

TABLE 8.1   The format of a writing test

SAMPLE WRITING TEST

Write a scene that involves two characters investigating a location and making a discovery that leads them to a second location. The scene should contain the following:

- A conversation
- A choice
- A short cinematic

You have a week to complete the test, but please don't spend more than one evening on it. Use a contemporary setting and language, but do **not** set it in the universe of any existing IP. The scene should be no more than 3–5 pages long, in standard screenplay format. You can provide additional materials such as flowcharts or character bios, but we will only assess your scene.

That's it! I consider this a reasonable writing test. It's one scene and one night, with no real incentive for spending more effort than that. Also, the IP restrictions make it clear that they're not trying to steal your work for their game. So, write with confidence.

WHAT DO STUDIOS LOOK FOR?

It's tempting to say, "good writing," but that's not all hiring managers want. Tests vary by studio and project, but they're all asking the same question: "Can you write for *our* game?"

By the time you're asked to take the test, they already know you can write well. What they don't know is if you can write the kind of games they make. That's what the test reveals. So do your research and make sure you know the house style, or your test will flop.

HOW CAN I TELL IF IT'S A SCAM?

Scam artists have swooped in like vultures to take advantage of lengthy writing tests. The scammers ask for a game mission as a "test," then say, "Hmm, it's hard to judge. Why don't you write another mission to help us decide?" So you write another "test" mission, but they still can't decide. So you write one more. Before you know it, you've written a third of their game. If they con enough people, they can get writing for an entire game. Scammers often say they'll pay you when you finish the "test," but vanish when you ask for the money. Many scam artists pretend they represent prestigious studios such as Bungie or Ubisoft. They trade on the studio's good reputation to trick you into doing work for them. And they keep pushing for more free work until you get suspicious or give up. It's unscrupulous as hell, but it happens all the time. So how do you avoid getting scammed?

Red Flags

You might think, "Eh, I'm not an idiot. I'd never fall for a scam," but you're wrong. It seems clumsy and obvious when I explain it, but I know seasoned writers who have been fooled. Scammers are convincing! It's what they do for a living. And, after months of rejections, you might be vulnerable and eager to believe someone values your writing. Keep your head and look for some warning signs:

- No reputable studio will ask you for money. Not for "application fees" or anything else. Never pay to take a test or submit an application.
- Check their email to see if the studio name is in the address. If someone emails from a personal address and claims to represent the studio, ask them to email from their work address.
- Some scammers establish "studios" that assemble entire games through fake tests. If they say they'll pay you, ask for half the money up front. If they refuse, then you refuse.
- If you take a paid "test" and they ask you to do additional work before getting paid, don't do it. Resist your sunk-cost impulse; scammers are counting on it. Always get payment for completed work before taking on more.

Fortunately, most studios aren't scammers. Applying to a AAA studio through their website is safe, and their writing test will be legit. Use common sense and remember that if an opportunity seems too good to be true, it probably is.

HOW DO I ACE THE WRITING TEST?

Here's the truth: most people don't. Sometimes what studios want isn't a good fit for you, and you'll struggle with the test. That's okay! You bomb some tests and ace others. Most of the time you fall somewhere in the middle and that's good enough. A lot depends on the project and your personal style. Knowing all that, here's how you can set yourself up for success.

Do Your Research

I've said it before, but it's worth repeating: know what kind of games you'll be writing for. Look at the company website and check the news to see what projects they're developing. If it's a just-announced title and there's no information about it, look at their other titles. You can get a pretty good sense of, say,

Supergiant's writing philosophies from their *Bastion, Transistor*, and *Hades* games. Then write your test in the studio style.

Follow the Instructions

Why would anyone ignore the test instructions? I wonder that too, but you'd be amazed by how many people just…do their own thing. Maybe they're mavericks, I don't know. But trust me, the instructions matter. If the test asks for "no more than five pages," don't write ten. We might be testing for brevity! If the test asks for a short conversation, don't write a long cinematic. Write what the test asks you to. And if you don't understand something, ask the recruiter for clarification! They want you to do well.

Don't Cheat!

Look, I get it. It's tough to write a good, sharp script in one night. Maybe your intentions were good, but something came up. You got food poisoning. Meemaw got sick. Your day job kept you late. Whatever it was, ask for more time if you need it. It's better to ask than to tweak an existing sample into kinda-sorta matching the test—or worse, outright send pages from a pre-written script. Studios can usually tell when you fudge the test. Do you think the job isn't worth the effort? Will you cut corners on your work if you get it? Is the writing even yours? Cheating raises questions, none of them good. Just take the test and do your best.

Minimize Risks

Writing tests are your chance to blow them away, so bring out your big guns. Show off your genius for witty banter or your slick narrative design skills. This isn't the place to try out new material or try a risky new authorial voice. Write what you *know* you're good at, and dazzle your readers.

Have Fun!

I'm not being sarcastic here. If you decide to take the test, you might as well enjoy it. Treat it as a fun writing exercise, and create something that entertains you. Then, however the test turns out, you've got a sample you like for your portfolio.

WHAT IF I BOMB THE WRITING TEST?

"You can't ace every test." Haha, just some wisdom from a puppet friend[1] of mine! It's a good, wholesome message though. You're competing with some of the best game writers in the world. Rejection doesn't mean your work was bad, it simply wasn't what this particular studio needed for this particular role. Chalk it up as good practice and keep going.

Ask for Feedback

I always write a few notes on tests about what worked and what didn't, but those notes don't always reach candidates. Ask for them! At worst, you'll get no notes or vague, high-level feedback. But you might get granular, insightful feedback that helps you understand the rejection. Use that feedback to improve your test as you turn it into a sample for your portfolio.

CAN I USE MY TESTS AS WRITING SAMPLES?

You better believe it. Also, if you were paid for the test, see if the company will let you list it as contract work.

HOW DO I TURN TESTS INTO SAMPLES?

Don't throw those tests into a drawer and never look at them again! With a few simple changes, writing tests become samples that really beef up your portfolio. But make sure you follow the rules.

File Off the Serial Numbers

Don't break your NDA! Get permission to put the test in your portfolio. Some places are fine with you sharing the work as-is, but some will ask you to scrub off any proprietary information.[2] Here's how you swap out IP-specific names for unconnected names:

- Bad: Elden Ring becomes Olden Ring. Kratos becomes Crator. Guardians become Guards. Come on now! That's way too obvious.
- Good: Elden Ring becomes The Ancients. Kratos becomes Monstra. Guardians become soldiers. Unless there are other identifying markers in the test, nobody will connect the new names to the originals.

Some studios ask you to remove any "signature narrative features" that might link your sample to their game. This means an unusual tone, setting, or plotline. But usually, it's okay to turn the test into a sample "in the style of" their published IPs. Ask yourself, "Could I have written this test as fanfic without knowing anything about the current project?" If the answer is yes, then you're probably safe.

Stay Inside the Lines

Can you post the entire test online, prompt included? Eh, I wouldn't. Unless the studio explicitly said you could, which is unlikely, that's a direct violation of your NDA. Don't risk it. Besides, posting the prompt is a dead giveaway that your sample was once a test and not a brilliant piece you dreamed up on your own. Why undermine your own work? A few simple changes keep it inside the NDA boundaries and let you post it with pride.

NOTES

1   "You and Your Special Powers." Threshold Kids, CONTROL. https://www.youtube.com/watch?v=lNNDcNJhIo0. Shout-out to my partners in crime, Clay Murphy, Mircea Purdea, and Heli Salomaa.
2   For an example of this, check out the story bible TOC in Chapter 14. I've scrubbed all IP-specific terms, so now it could be from any of the games I worked on.

The Dotted Line

9

Congratulations! You made it through the hiring process! You sailed past the test and impressed your interviewers. The company wants you to join their team. At this point, you should receive an offer letter.

WHAT'S IN AN OFFER LETTER?

A standard offer letter defines the role you're being offered:

- Job title (make sure this is correct!)
- Job description
- Length of contract and start date (optional, but short-term work often includes it)
- Salary or hourly pay rate
- Benefits (PTO, health insurance, pension, annual bonuses)
- Perks (stock options, company apartment, gym membership, free snacks)
- One-time perks (relocation allowance, signing bonus)

If you've already discussed your salary needs with the recruiter, the offer should be no surprise. But even if the amount is exactly what you expected, hold up! This isn't the end of the hiring process; it's the start of salary negotiations.

HOW DO I KNOW IT'S A GOOD OFFER?

Don't go with your gut feeling or assume it's the "best they can do." Go gather some data.

DOI: 10.1201/9781003282259-10

Salary Information

In California, studios must include a salary range in all job posts. This is a new policy and it's fantastic news for candidates. Now you can see what the high and low salaries are for the role. Experience, seniority, and craft specializations can place you higher or lower in that range, of course, but at least you have solid figures to work with. Along with the posted range, check out Glassdoor, the many games industry spreadsheets[1] that float around social media and, above all, ask someone who's doing the job you want!

Cost of Living

Game writers living in the EU are gobsmacked by the salaries our US counterparts make. They are sometimes 2–3 times higher! But when you factor in the cost of living for San Francisco versus Helsinki, you'll realize that they're comparable. Pop some figures into Numbeo and see how far that jaw-dropping USD 125k salary gets you in San Francisco.

More

If you're making what your peers are making, you have all the benefits you need, and you can live comfortably in that region, then it's probably a good offer. But you should still ask for more.

HOW DO I NEGOTIATE A BETTER OFFER?

When that offer letter arrives, your first instinct will be to shoot back an enthusiastic "yes!" and get on board as soon as you can. Stop right there! *Never accept the first offer.* The effects of this salary negotiation will ripple across your career for years to come. So be smart, know your worth, and figure out your counteroffer.

Never Go First

Here's your golden rule for salary negotiations: never name a figure first. If you do, you're almost guaranteed to lowball yourself. If the recruiter point-blank asks, "What salary do you want?" Respond with, "What's the range for this role?" *Never answer with a number.* If the job application has a field that asks for your desired salary, leave the field blank or write "negotiable." If the field only accepts numbers, then research the range before answering. But dodge that bullet for as long as possible.

Know Your Worth

Before sending a counteroffer, remind yourself how awesome you are. Glance over the resume and cover letter you sent. Wow, look at all those skills and accomplishments! The studio is damn lucky to get you! *That's* the energy you should negotiate with. Don't be intimidated or afraid they'll withdraw the offer. Finding the right person for a role is enormously expensive and time consuming. The studio wants to bring you on and close out that job post, believe me. As long as your counteroffer isn't absurdly high (pro tip: don't ask for more than the CEO makes), they'll try to work out a happy compromise.

Negotiating Bias

Haggling for a decent wage is already tough, but women, BIPOC, and other marginalized devs have it tougher. We walk the razor edge between being likable and assertive while fighting to be paid the same amount as our non-marginalized peers. It's exhausting and frustrating and you'll be tempted to settle for less than you want. Don't do it! Fight for what you know you're worth. Try reading Tara Wheeler's *Minute-Zero in the Gender Pay Gap*[2] before entering negotiations. It's short, sensible, and it gives you a script to use during negotiations. Good luck!

SHOULD I WORK FOR EXPOSURE?

The first thing I tell my mentees is "never work for free." The second thing I tell my mentees is "never work for free." Here, I mapped it out for you (Figure 9.1).

You'll get offers to do work "for exposure" or for a game credit without receiving any wages, and that's slightly more complicated. In those cases, you should weigh the value of what you're getting from it against what you're

FIGURE 9.1   Should I work for free flowchart.

putting in. Helping to run your local game jam so you can put that on your resume? Probably worth it. Writing a 30-page instruction manual for your friend's indie game? They should pay you. The Writer's Guild of Great Britain has a more detailed flowchart on their website[3] to help you with nuanced decisions. But generally, don't work for free.

WHAT SALARY SHOULD I ASK FOR?

A good one, haha. But seriously, you decide what a "good" salary looks like for you. Start with the research you did to assess the first salary offer. Get numbers from the studio website, Glassdoor, salary spreadsheets, or from other game writers. This gives you a salary range to work with.

Make A Budget

Take your salary range and head to Numbeo to see the cost of living in the studio's area. Use their data to work up an estimated budget of your monthly expenses (Table 9.1).

TABLE 9.1   An estimated monthly budget

EXPENSE	COST[a]
Rent and Food	1,800
Transportation	150
Candles	700
Bills (electricity, phone, cable, etc.)	250
Debt (student loans, credit cards, etc.)	300
Other (entertainment, subscriptions, etc.)	250
TOTAL	**3,450**

[a] I used random numbers for this example budget. Don't judge me! Unless you're @dril.

Find Your Floor and Ceiling

Add up the numbers and you've got your salary floor. That's the rock bottom of your budget. Don't go below it if you want to survive! But you want to do more than just scrape by, let's figure out the top end of that range. Add costs for small luxuries like travel, books, and more candles! Add the amount you want to set aside as savings. Add a little more as a negotiating buffer, and voila! There's your ceiling. This is the number you'll shoot for. Even if you haggle down a bit, you'll still end up with a higher salary than they originally offered.

Shoot Your Shot

Now you can write back to the studio, tell them how excited you are to work with them, and present your counteroffer. That will kick off the negotiations. You'll probably go back and forth a few times before you agree on a number. Have faith in your research and don't go below your floor. Don't forget to negotiate the benefits and perks too! If the studio can't increase your pay, maybe they can give you a better title or a signing bonus. Stand your ground, and don't be afraid to push for what you need.

If They Say No

If they can't meet your well-researched and competitive salary request, then you should probably walk away. Or take it and immediately start looking for a better-paying job.

If They Say Yes

Good job, you. You've set yourself up for a successful career. Pat yourself on the back and sign that offer letter!

DO I NEED A LAWYER?

Nah. Unless you're signing a contract for intellectual property rights or you're a freelance contractor, you can do fine on your own. Organizations like the WGGB offer contract reviews as a membership benefit, but they don't have the time to go over every section and clause with you or negotiate on your behalf. For that, you would need to hire a lawyer.

WHAT'S A REASONABLE RATE FOR A LAWYER?

Review of a standard contract should cost the equivalent of a few thousand dollars in your local currency.

WHAT SHOULD I LOOK FOR IN A CONTRACT?

When you read through your contract, look for two things:

- Is everything we agreed on here?
- Is anything I don't agree with here?

Is Everything We Agreed on Here?

This means checking for typos or errors. If you accepted a senior writer role and the contract says only "writer," correct that mistake. Remember, the contract is your proof of agreement. Check that all those benefits and perks you negotiated so hard for are there in writing.

Is Anything I Don't Agree With Here?

If you didn't hire a lawyer, read your contract carefully. Read every line and make sure you understand what its implications are. If you see a clause that's too restrictive, push back on it. If the company says no, keep pushing back. You won't win every battle, but I've always found studios amenable to reasonable adjustments.

BEFORE YOU SIGN

Signing a contract means you're legally bound by its contents, so make sure you agree with everything in it. Don't sign it until you understand what everything means. Ask questions, request changes, and take an active role in adjusting the contract to your satisfaction. *Never sign a document you don't understand.*

Clauses to Watch Out For

Here are the key points I always make sure I understand:

- **Salary** – How much do you make? When do you get paid? How do you get paid? Do you get overtime or wage-based perks?
- **Bonuses** – What are the requirements to receive a bonus? If it's profit-based, what is the formula for determining it? When are bonuses handed out?
- **Notice period** – If you decide to leave, how far in advance do you need to notify the company? If they lay you off or (horrors) fire you, how much advance notice do they need to give you?
- **Raises and Promotions** – Are you guaranteed an annual salary review or raise? When do you qualify for a promotion?
- **Title** – Make sure your official title is what you agreed upon.
- **Credits** – Some studios have a blanket policy that if you leave before ship, then you get "Special Thanks" and that's it. There are no industry-wide rules for credits, and devs have almost no recourse when there's a problem or a dispute, beyond the good will of the studio. Get a guarantee in writing from the start.

- **Intellectual Property** – Another sticky wicket in many AAA contracts. The gist of it is that anything you create while working for the company belongs to the company. As a writer, that means anything you write or create. I've never seen this clause enforced, but it's a frightening thing to have in your contract. If you see this clause and have side projects, ask for a deed of variation.
- **Relocation Pay** – If you're moving for this job, you should negotiate a relocation package that covers all your needs. You should never pay for the cost of visa paperwork or moving fees on your own. If a company wants you to relocate, they should pay for it.
- **Signing Bonus** – This is a one-time payment usually offered to entice you away from another studio or job offer. If your salary offer was low, try to make it up here.
- **Noncompete clauses** – aka "restrictions after termination." Basically, they're rules for what you can do and who you can work for after you leave a company. These clauses can be quite limiting, but I've had good luck pushing back on them.

Unreasonable Clauses

If any part of your contract makes it impossible for you to earn a living, then it's probably not legally valid.[4] You have to be able to earn a living.

CAN I WORK ON SIDE PROJECTS?

Even if you have no current side projects, it's worth finding out the studio policy. You never know what opportunities will come your way in the future. You might work on an indie game or become a streamer. You might randomly decide to write a book of game-writing career advice. Whatever side hustle you pick up, know what your options are.

Deed of Variation

If the studio correctly perceives that your mini-painting book is no competition for their video games, they'll have you sign a deed of variation. This is essentially a short addendum to your contract. A deed of variation says that whatever you produce as result of your side project belongs to you. That might seem obvious or silly, but if there's a clause in your main contract giving the studio ownership of any work you do while employed for them—any work at all—then you need to carve out an exception. Most AAA companies don't have a problem with side projects, as long as you run it by them first.

SIGNY SIGN

Once everybody's happy with the contract, it's autograph time! The studio will send you the adjusted contract to sign. Read through it carefully one last time and then pull out your pen. Or keyboard. You'll probably receive it through an electronic signature service like DocuSign, so simply follow the instructions and download the signed copy when you're finished. Make sure you get a final, signed copy for your records and bam! You're signed, sealed, and ready to go.

NOTES

1   Karr, Evva. "Global GameDev Salary Database 2021." http://bit.ly/GameDevSalaries 2021.

2   Wheeler, Tarah. "Minute-Zero in the Gender Pay Gap." Medium. Last updated 25 June 2015. Minute-Zero in the Gender Pay Gap|by Tarah Wheeler |Tarah Wheeler|Medium

3   https://writersguild.org.uk/wp-content/uploads/2021/12/WGGB-A4-Video games-6.12.21.pdf

4   Huge thanks to Pete Lewin, Senior Associate at Wiggin LLP, for much of the advice in this chapter. I interviewed Pete for my *Game Writing Guide* in May 2022.

Press Start

10

Hey, look at you! You're a game dev now. Time to pop some bubbly and celebrate! Maybe you landed your dream job; maybe it's just the first rung of a tall ladder. Either way, you want to start off strong.

WHAT SHOULD I DO ON MY FIRST DAY?

The first thing you should do is chill. Nobody expects you to jump in and start proving yourself immediately. So, relax, breathe, and follow these pointers:

- **Meet your team**. You met them during interviews, but now you can have a nice chat and get to know them better. Learn their roles, and how the team collaborates.
- **Learn the studio**: Take a studio tour to learn where everything is. Which conference room is closest to your desk? Where's the break room? Where do different departments sit? Where are the free snacks? Learn all the important information for working in an office day to day. If you work remotely, you'll probably spend some quality time with IT getting set up.
- **Learn the social media policy**. Before you post pictures of your new swag on Insta, check the rules. Don't be that person who gets chewed out their first day for violating company policy. There are strict rules about what you can say online, especially if you have the studio or project name in your bio. Make sure you know what's acceptable.

Your first day on the job will be a whirlwind of introductions and paperwork. In AAA, you'll have meetings with various departments to learn about your health insurance, PTO, pay schedule, and other important information. Don't worry! They'll tell you where to go and what to do. As long as you understand everything you sign, you're golden.

DOI: 10.1201/9781003282259-11

WHAT SHOULD I DO MY FIRST WEEK?

After the first few days, you'll be left on your own. Your lead may have assignments for you, so jump right on those. But here are some other tasks you should lock down right away.

- **Meet your extended team**: Get to know people on the teams you'll collaborate with. Quest Design, Art, Audio, Level Design, QA, Localization—know who to contact with specific questions and how their workflows fit into yours.
- **Learn the virtual office**: Even if you work on site or hybrid, it's important to learn the virtual layout. Ransack the company website to learn the important links and procedures. How do you book an online meeting? What does your team structure look like? All that good virtual stuff.
- **Learn company policy**: It's more than social media rules! Make sure you understand procedures for getting paid, expense reimbursements, reporting problems, and other life maintenance issues. Read the company handbook cover to cover. You might never look at it again, but know what's in there for future reference.
- **Know your probation requirements**: Probation periods are increasingly common in games these days. They last from a few weeks to as long as six months! During that time, either party can end the relationship at any time with no penalty. Probation periods are stressful if you like the job and want to stay. The best way to alleviate that stress is knowing exactly what's expected of you. Have your lead write up a list of probation goals, and focus on achieving them. Check in with your lead for a progress report every few weeks. Seeing your progress is the best antidote for anxiety.
- **Read *all* the project documentation**. I mean everything, from lore wikis to design documents. I've started on projects so early that narrative "documentation" was a pitch deck and a hopeful smile, but most places will have a pile of docs for you to read. Take that deep dive! The game will change over time, of course, but know where it is when you start. And ask questions. Nobody expects you to know anything the first week, so take advantage of that fact.
- **Give feedback**: After reading your team's documentation, write up some feedback. You're seeing the project with unjaded eyes, so they'll want to know what you think. Keep your feedback constructive. If you haven't learned how to give good feedback yet, now's the time to learn.

HANDLING FEEDBACK

We're in a creative industry, so learning to give and receive thoughtful feedback is a core skill. Most writing job posts contain some version of "don't be precious" about your work, which translates to "handle feedback well." But *giving* constructive feedback is also important. Many AAA companies offer feedback training, so sign up if it's offered. It's valuable to know what *that studio* thinks good feedback looks like. If there are no classes, try some of these resources:

- *Radical Candor* by Kim Scott
- Let's Talk About Feedback[1]
- Improving Critique of Game Projects with Expert and Peer Feedback[2]

Giving feedback with diplomacy and receiving it with grace are essential skills for writers. You'll use them daily throughout your career, so you might as well learn how early.

So, I listed more stuff than you can do in a week, but that's okay! You've got time to learn and get off to a good start.

HOW DO I KNOW WHAT WORK TO DO?

Once you've mastered the basics and you're all settled in, what next? Oh, nothing much. Just *actually doing the job*. But honestly, that's the easy part. Your responsibilities vary by development stage, so know where the project is on that timeline.

Depending on who you ask, there are anywhere from three to seven stages of the game development process. Officially, the flow looks something this:

Ideation (Planning) > Preproduction > Production > Testing > Pre-Launch > Launch > Post Production (and Live Service)

Or, more simply, preproduction > production > post production. Game writers do the bulk of our work in prepro and production, so this book focuses on those two stages.

In preproduction, you'll write external documents: a story guide or "bible," story treatments, story summaries, casting briefs, and pitches. Later on, in production, you'll focus more on in-game elements like barks, readables, UI text, screenplays, bios, trailers, etc. There's no room in this tiny handbook to go into detail on those but I recommend *The Game Narrative Toolbox* for advice crafting those essential game elements.

WHAT IS PREPRODUCTION WORK LIKE?

AAA game writing is great because every day brings new challenges—but that's also its downside. In prepro, your workday is relaxed and blue-sky creative. You'll write pitches, brainstorm plotlines, and carve out the shape of the world and story. Now's when you prototype narrative features (like conversation systems and readables) and start pondering which actors should bring your key characters to life. You'll be asked to make a line count estimate. It will be wildly off, but that's expected. Prepro is more about approximations and laying foundations. You're making a "blueprint" of the project that the team will turn into a playable game during production.

WHAT IS PRODUCTION WORK LIKE?

Production is where it all gets real. You take the ideas and plans, that "blueprint" from prepro, and you build it. Many writers prefer this stage because it's where they practice their craft and do on-the-page writing. In story-driven games, narrative enters production before the other teams. We lay the track for the rest of the project to follow. This can be a chaotic process if you're not working far enough ahead of the other disciplines. Picture laying the track as the train races down it. But if you've planned well and stay on target, you'll finish before other teams do and spend your last year polishing lines, working with QA and Loc, and planning DLC or sequels.

WHAT'S A WRITER'S DAY TO DAY LIKE?

You'll have individual assignments to focus on day to day, but some tasks are ubiquitous. Here are some of the Tetris blocks that fill a writer's calendar (Table 10.1).

TABLE 10.1   Tasks in a game writer's daily schedule

• Meetings/collaborations	• Playthroughs
• Spreadsheets	• Recording sessions
• Reviews and feedback	• Implementation
• Research	• Pitches and presentations
• Writing	• Revisions

These daily tasks are where the work gets done. Add it up, and you've got a shippable game. On your march to completion, you'll pass some key development milestones:

- **Greenlight Build** – The name says it all. It's the game build[3] that gets the "greenlight," the go-ahead, from your publisher or funder.
- **Vertical Slice** – It's like taking a core sample of the game. You see a small section of the game and game systems, but not all of them and not complete versions of them.
- **Demo** – They're highly polished sections of the larger game, usually a small region or single mission. They're designed to impress the public or press and give them a feel for what the completed game will be like.
- **Alpha** – This definition varies by studio, but think of it as the rough draft of the game. All the important ideas are in there, but they still need a lot of work to shine.
- **Beta** – Open to the general public or "closed" to all but a few invited players. A more polished version of the game for active testing. It's still rough around the edges, but it's close to ready at this stage.
- **Gold Master** – When a game "goes gold" or is approved for publication. In ye olden times, the game was burned onto a gold disk hence the name. This is the game you ship.

There are other milestones such as Content Complete and Pre-Alpha, but this overview is enough to get you started. Writers have their own flow and deadlines too. Final Scriptlock is the important one, because there are no changes to writing after that point.

Nowadays, there's no rest after a game "goes gold." The main team keeps forging ahead with bug fixes and updates, while a smaller group splinters off to work on DLC. Sometimes teams try to do both, which makes for a frantic, finishing crunch. Games as a Service (GaaS) have an ongoing live component with frequent content updates, so there's plenty more work to do after the game is out there and (hopefully!) a success.

HOW DO I WORK IN A WRITERS' ROOM?

If you're lucky, your studio will have a big enough narrative team to have writers' rooms. Games borrowed this term from TV, and they're run in similar ways. I call them "story summits" at my studios, and they involve going to an offsite location to hammer out the details of a story. These brainstorm sessions are exhausting, rewarding, and creatively fertile experiences. Unless you're leading the discussion ("running the show"), your job is easy. Simply show up and be creative. There's an "anything goes" feeling to a good writers' room, where there truly are no dumb ideas. Your meh idea might spark someone else's amazing idea. So say it! The most important thing here is to be enthusiastic, respectful of your fellow writers, and to (try to) stay on topic. Other than that, have fun!

HOW DO I GET HEARD?

When your job is communicating ideas, what happens when you're silenced? You get talked over, your ideas get stolen, someone rephrases what you just said, you're talked down to like you're stupid, or you just don't feel heard. I've been in all these situations before, and they're frustrating as hell. Here are my strategies:

- Document the incidents and draw attention to them. When you have some specific examples, go to your lead and ask for solutions. If not your lead, then your colleagues, HR, or an online support group. (If you're not comfortable talking to anyone at work about it, you might have bigger problems than just being talked over.)

- Confront people in the moment. If someone steals my idea in a meeting, I immediately jump in and say, "Yes! That's exactly what I meant! Thank you for rephrasing it…" That returns credit to me, and I seize the opportunity to clarify my thought.
- If you're being talked over or silenced routinely, a problem especially experienced by marginalized folks, try using an app like GenderEQ to measure how much everyone's really talking. Then go to your lead or HR for help, *armed with data.* That last point is important! You always want to argue from a place of fact versus other people's perceptions or opinions.

Most of these solutions require assertiveness and help from allies. And getting their help means proving the problem exists. Documenting helps and is especially important when being talked down to, where there's usually a wider pattern of disrespect.

HOW DO I DEAL WITH IMPOSTER SYNDROME?

I hate to tell you this, but some of the most accomplished people I know suffer from Imposter Syndrome. I don't know the cure for it. And quite frankly, I'm a little suspicious of writers who don't have occasional doubts about their work. It's healthy to wonder if your work has room for improvement. And when you're just starting out and meeting your heroes, it's natural to feel intimidated. But if it interferes with your work and prevents you from contributing, try this: start a Praise Folder on your desktop. Every time someone says something nice about your work or performance, even if it's a short message on Slack, snip it and put it into the folder. Whenever you doubt yourself, go look at the accolades you've earned. Accept that people think you're doing good work—even if you don't think so. That folder of accomplishments will also come in veeery handy when it comes time to ask for a raise or promotion.

HOW DO I GET TO THE NEXT LEVEL?

Whoa, whoa! It's your first day, and I'm already saying you should level up? Darn right I am. Start your planning from Day One. Learn your studio's hierarchy and what every role does. Map out your path from your current role to your dream job. How can you get there?

Get Direction

Form a relationship with your lead and get them actively involved in your career goals. Ask for mentoring. Get them on board, and they'll be your biggest ally. They can clear obstacles in your path and fight for resources you need. Be upfront about your aspirations and how they can support you.

Training

Dig through the studio's resources to learn what training they offer. Ubisoft has a wealth of tutorials and online instruction you can take on your own time. If your studio doesn't have a mini-university, see if they'll pay for outside training. Research seminars and online workshops and ask your company to fund them. (Here's where your lead can help.) Most studios are happy to pay for training that has obvious practical benefits for your work. But hey, if they won't, guess what? Nothing's stopping you learning on your own. Check back to Chapter Two for options.

Mentoring

These early years are when you need mentoring the most. I hope this book helps answer the big questions, but you'll also want someone you can go to with smaller problems. Ideally, that person is your lead. But when your lead *is* the problem, you need a real mentor. Find someone who's doing the job you want, at your studio or in the wider industry, and ask them if they'd be willing to answer a few questions about their work. Most folks are happy to.

Keep Improving

Some writers get their first job and go limp on networking. They've made it, they're in, they can relax now, right? No! Don't throw away the network you worked so hard to build. Now's the time to ramp up your networking. Connect with your new colleagues and have them introduce you to their friends. Seize every opportunity to speak on panels and give presentations. Marginalized devs should seek out any orgs or ERGs[4] that can offer advice tailormade for their needs. Find a community of people and friends to help you. Trust me, your journey through this industry will be much easier if you do.

NOTES

1   "Let's Talk About Feedback." Peet Cooper, GDC 2018. https://gdcvault.com/play/1025175/Let-s-Talk-About
2   "Improving Critique of Game Projects with Expert and Peer Feedback." Jessica Hammer & Martin Pichlmair, GDC 2018. https://gdcvault.com/play/1024966/Improving-Critique-of-Game-Projects
3   Build = version of the game.
4   ERG = Employee Resource Group. Internal special-interest groups, such as Pride, POC, or women's groups.

Hurdles

11

Your first year in the industry whizzes by. The novelty of studio life wears off, and you barely blink when you pass Spyro cosplay in the hall. Now's when you'll get antsy for improvement: a raise, promotion, or even just some noise-canceling headphones. Or maybe you have more serious issues to contend with because, let's face it, your game-writing career won't always be sunshine and roses.

HOW CAN I WORK IN THIS ENVIRONMENT?

Open offices are hellish for writers. There you are, struggling to think of the perfect word, while the engineer behind you chatters away and fills your head with hundreds of wrong words. It's maddening, but it's easy to fix.

- **Short term**: If you need to focus near a deadline, try booking a conference room for day-long writing sessions. Set a no-talking rule and invite your whole team to write peacefully together. Or ask if you can work from home (or offline) a day or two.
- **Long-term**: If it's a serious problem, like migraines from the office lights or sensory overload from all the open-office activity (I feel for you, my neurodivergent friends!), then have a chat with HR about accommodations.

One company asked for a doctor's note when I requested a standing desk, but most places are happy to help adjust the ergonomics of your workstation. I've seen accommodations for dyslexia, hypersomnia, autism, fibromyalgia, Tourette's, among dozens of other conditions. Studios want you to be comfortable so you can do good work. Ask for help before your problem becomes a crisis.

DOI: 10.1201/9781003282259-12

HOW DO I OVERCOME WRITER'S BLOCK?

If this is your first job as a professional writer, you'll quickly learn there's a big difference between writing on your own and writing to a deadline. The pressure can be exhilarating or it can be paralyzing. Experience tells me that "writer's block" is another way to say "I'm afraid people won't like my work." You're so worried about your work failing the standard that you freeze up and can't get anything out. Everyone's got their own method for breaking through the block, but here's what *I'd* do in your situation.

- Talk to my lead about my fears. Are they valid? Am I really the worst writer in the history of the world? If so, how can I improve?
- Get a garbage draft out. Seriously. Write the clunky, pun-tastic, bad version of whatever you're trying to create and get it out of your system. There's no pressure when you're *trying* to write badly, right? Once it's out, laugh at it, then start editing. Pinpoint why it's so bad and start fixing those bad bits. Before long, you've turned that garbage draft into something halfway decent. It's not far from there to good, so keep editing!
- Trick yourself. When I'm blocked, I tell myself that I'm going to write a little outline. That's not *real* writing; it's just a list of the points I want to make, for no eyes but my own. Then I expand on that list a bit. Then a bit more. Before I know it, I've got paragraphs of writing that I can stitch together into a full draft. And all without doing any writing (wink, wink).

HOW DO I ASK FOR A RAISE OR PROMOTION?

This one's easy! Bring the receipts. Go into your Praise File and take a good hard look at everything you've accomplished at the studio. Write up those accomplishments in a nice letter, add a line or two about what more you'd like to do, and you're all set. I won't spend much time on this topic because a quick online search will net you tons of advice. But here are a few extra pointers.

Procedure

Find out the procedure for requesting promotions and raises at your studio. Is there a specific window for reviews and advancement? Should you email your lead or submit a request to HR? Follow the proper steps.

Performance

Keep your request factual and performance based. Focus on what you've accomplished and how well you've done it. I've seen some promotion requests that are simply "I've been here for a while so it's time to promote me." While that's definitely an argument to make, back it up with some persuasive accomplishments. "I led the feature design for all key readables and delivered them ahead of schedule." This is especially important for raises. Remind them of your value.

Keywords

For promotions, look at the description for the role you want. Now, break it down the same way you did the job post back in Chapter 3. Pull out the keywords and include them in your email to your line manager. Treat this like you're applying for the role and persuade them you're the best person for that job.

The Next Level

Prove you're not just doing great work at your current level; you're already doing the work of the *next* level and doing it well. The raise or promotion is just a formality.

Get Feedback

This is important! If you get turned down, make sure you understand why. Get clear feedback about what you need to change or improve. Address those areas over time, then try again.

COST-OF-LIVING ADJUSTMENT

If you don't get a raise for your stellar performance, you should still receive an annual adjustment for cost-of-living increases. If your living expenses go up and your pay doesn't, you've effectively taken a pay cut. Many devs end up studio hopping when their wages don't keep up with inflation—or competition.

HOW DO I MANAGE MY MANAGER?

If you're lucky, you'll have a good lead. They'll prepare you for the next step in your career and guide you along that path with focused critique and actionable feedback. If you have a lead like that, ignore this section! But for all other leads—the bad, incompetent, indifferent, or overwhelmed—you'll have to help them help you. This is called "managing up."

Show Some Empathy

If your lead isn't giving you guidance or support, stop and ask yourself why. It's easy to slap that "bad" label on them when you're frustrated, but are they really? I'm not here to defend leads who leave their teams to flounder, ignore cries for help, or worse. There are some awful leads out there, I know. But usually your lead is simply buried in work and can't find time to help. If that's the case, you can help *them*.

Know Thyself

Your first step is to understand your own process. Every writer has their own way of working. Maybe you write better with loose deadlines. Maybe you need written feedback after every draft. Some writers thrive with detailed direction and extensive oversight. Personally, I like my lead to set clear parameters and then free me to do whatever I want within those boundaries. Make sure you understand your needs because you'll have to articulate them to your manager.

Tactics

Once you've defined your needs, figure out what works best for you *and* your lead. If they're overwhelmed, you might end up doing most of the "management" yourself. Set up short daily check-ins to get clarity on your tasks. Start your emails with a summary of work that you've done and *why your lead should care*. I've outlined my own sprint schedule and created a bullet-pointed list of tasks to review and check off with my lead as they're accomplished. The work gets done, your lead stays updated, and you get their guidance to do good work.

WHAT IF MY MANAGER WON'T HELP?

It's unusual for managers to push back when you're asking for guidance (they want you to get the work done too), but it happens. Stick with it! Be clear that you're happy to do the work; you just don't understand how they want it. Also, absolutely push back on your workload. If you have too much work and you can't get it done within the expected timeframe or to the expected quality level, let your lead know right away. Don't wait until it's too late and you miss your deadline.

If you can't get the help you need after several tries and your work is suffering, send up flares! Talk to your team about their strategies. Talk to your lead's lead. If you think it's a personality issue, go to HR. But don't suffer in silence. Go around your manager to actively seek the help you need to do your best work.

DO I HAVE TO CRUNCH?

There comes a time in every game writer's life when they're asked to crunch. I won't go into the arguments surrounding this issue, but I encourage you to read up on the physical and mental stress crunch causes. Research shows that crunch in limited stints is effective, but beyond four weeks it stops working and becomes actively harmful. If you're asked to crunch, do three things before agreeing:

1. Check your contract to see if you're obligated to crunch and what the penalties are if you say no. If you refuse to crunch after signing a contract saying you will, you're in a precarious position.

Technically, you're violating your contract. If you're obligated to crunch, see if you're entitled to extra pay or bonuses for it and skip to Step 3.

2. Talk to your team and lead about crunch. Share some articles. Try to get everyone on the same page. Crunch often comes with the soft pressure of not wanting to let your team down. If you refuse to crunch, refuse as a team. It carries more weight.

3. If you decide to crunch—or if you feel you have no choice—then try to limit the duration. Agree to a few weeks of crunch, at most. Point to all the studies that show crunch stops being effective after a certain point, and in fact gives diminishing returns.

HOW DO I STOP BURNOUT?

Crunch long enough and you'll burn out. That makes sense, right? But it might surprise you to know burnout frequently comes without overwork. It can come from having no control over your work or schedule. Or having so much work that you can't do a good job. If you're a creative person, it might come from having no creative outlet or doing unfulfilling work. Burnout can ambush you. You think you're living a healthy life with reasonable hours and *wham*! It drops on you like a Looney Tunes anvil.

There are some phenomenal talks about burnout available for free in the GDC Vault, so watch those to understand what you're dealing with:

- Occupational Burnout in Games: Causes, Impact, and Solutions[1]
- Battling Burnout: The Side Project Ritual[2]
- An Evidence-Based Mental Health Model for Game Developers[3]

HELP! I'M BEING MISTREATED. WHAT DO I DO?

If the problem is severe—harassment, abuse, death-march crunch—get out. No job is worth that kind of treatment. If it's not a critical situation, but it's more than you can handle on your own, then document, document, document! I keep a bullet journal of my workdays. The entries are short, high-level notes about what happened that day and how I'm feeling. It's a great way to demonstrate a pattern of problematic behavior. Once you've documented the pattern, go to HR with your records. If you make your case to them and nothing happens or they dismiss your fears, then you'll have to look for help elsewhere. Talk to an outside source like a union, support group, or legal aid. But don't "just put up with it." You have options.

HOW DO I DEAL WITH DISCRIMINATION?

If you're being discriminated against, then again, my best advice is to document it. Write down what happened, note the date and time, get witnesses, talk about it with friends. If it's serious enough, go to HR with your evidence and ask them to intervene. However, we've all seen the headlines, and clearly discrimination still happens. If HR can't or won't intervene, then your only options are to leave or find help through outside support groups, your guild or union, or legal aid centers in your region.

WHEN SHOULD I GO TO HR?

They get a bad rap, but Human Resources is your main stop for certain problems. Not all problems, but many. They also have a legal obligation to assist members of protected classes.

• Sex/Gender	• Religion
• Age	• Pregnancy
• Race	• Marital status
• Disability	• Veteran status
• National origin	• Genetic information

If you're being treated poorly because you have a disability or you're pregnant or because you're pagan, you *must* involve HR. Go even if you think it's pointless. Give them a chance. HR shines when they can signpost you to training, support, benefits, and other, well, resources. Sometimes, however, the help you need is beyond their purview. In those cases, don't hesitate to reach out to ERGs, your union or guild, industry SIGs, friends and family, the police, or legal aid to get the help you need. But try HR first. Then at least you tried the proper channel before seeking outside help, right?

HOW DO I HANDLE STUDIO POLITICS?

The same passion that got you into the industry will also get you into creative disagreements. But you can't fight for everything, so choose your "hills to die on" carefully. As you gain experience, you'll learn what hurts the story and what you can let slide. Weigh each problem that arises and decide if it's worth going to the mat for. It's easy to get a reputation as "difficult" or a "trouble-maker" if you challenge people too often. This is especially true for women, BIPOC, and other underrepresented groups. This was almost cartoonishly illus-trated for me early in my career, when a male colleague shouted, threw papers, and slammed his fist on the table after we received some bad news. I followed his response by speaking sharply and raising my voice. Guess who was told to "calm down"? You got it. I've since learned to walk away from those heated discussions and put my thoughts into writing when I've cooled down. And experience has taught me when it's not worth fighting over in the first place.

Allies

If you decide to stick to your guns and fight for a character or feature that mat-ters to you, you'll need allies to fight with you. Allies don't have to be your friends; they simply need to have the same goal as you. Understand what's in it for both of you and work together to achieve it. Team up to get what you want. Strategize! Achieve your goal. Then go back to business as usual.

Enemies

Society conditions us, especially women, to soothe other people's feelings, "play nice," and not rock the boat. Forget all that! Don't be afraid to make enemies. If you stand for anything, if you stand up for yourself, you'll make enemies. Social media has taught me that some people will find fault with any-thing you say or do—no matter how innocuous or diplomatic You can't avoid it, so don't worry about it. That's not permission to go out and be a jerk for no reason, but free yourself from the prison of always being "nice."

Find Your Community

I interviewed dozens of game devs for my books and heard stories of astonishing heartbreak and courage. One unifying message stood above all the others: find your community. Find a group of people to bounce ideas off, to support you, advise you, encourage you, and reassure you that you're not a loser when things fall apart. Find people who believe in you to counteract all the voices that will tell you you're bad. You'll make friends with colleagues in the trenches, but it's more than that natural camaraderie. Find people who understand you and support your goals. People that you can be *you* around. Having those friends, that community, is your best support for a long career.

Even the brightest and happiest careers will hit obstacles like those in this chapter. Maybe it's something minor like needing a new desk, or maybe it's a five-alarm career crisis. Turn to your community for help. They'll remind you why you're here and help you over the hurdles. They make every obstacle you face easier to overcome.

NOTES

1   Raffael Boccamazzo, et al. GDC 2023. https://gdcvault.com/play/1029254/Occupational-Burnout-in-Games-Causes
2   Laralyn McWilliams. GDC Summer 2020. https://gdcvault.com/play/1026779/Battling-Burnout-The-Side-Project
3   Jennifer Hazel. GDC 2018. https://gdcvault.com/play/1024903/An-Evidence-Based-Mental-Health

Running the Show

12

By the time you become a lead, you've seen the full rainbow of management styles, from good to bad, to what the heck. You're ready to jump in and be the best lead your team has ever seen! But sometimes a promotion comes out of the blue. There's a family tragedy, a tantalizing offer from another studio, or Life Just Happens—and a lead role opens unexpectedly. If you're catapulted into sudden leadership, don't panic! Running a three-ring circus is easier than it seems.

WHAT DOES A LEAD DO?

Remember my table of roles and experience waaay back in Chapter 1? Go take another peek at it. Notice how the responsibilities balloon once you're a lead? Yeah. That happens. Junior through senior, the bulk of your tasks are the same. You'll learn to work with less oversight and you'll own more significant pieces of the story, but the work itself doesn't vary much. But once you put that lead hat on, your focus switches from you to the team and project as a whole. It's a major perspective shift.

When You're the Lead

The leap from senior to lead can be tough if you haven't been trained in the management side of things. You'll have new responsibilities you've never done before. Here's a small sample:

DOI: 10.1201/9781003282259-13

Line Management	Hiring	Line Count Estimates
Check-ins and reviews	Run a writers' room	Story bible or macro
Schedule & roadmap	Training	Style guide
Tasking	Tracking deliverables	Casting briefs

You'll also be responsible for team morale and well-being, with all the little mental and emotional check-ins that keep your reports happy and productive. And don't forget your creative responsibilities: realizing the story vision, setting the writing standard for your team through examples, and even writing sections of the game. It's two roles in one! But your top priority is always your team.

HOW DO I KEEP TRACK OF EVERYTHING?

My friend, you're about to discover a brave new world of paperwork. You have to align the team's tasks with project-wide roadmaps and deliverable schedules. It's tough to keep tabs on everything with deadlines and deliverables shifting all the time, but it's critical that you do. Jira or ADO can track tasks and bugs, but you'll probably want a visualization or calendar on top of that. I love a good old-fashioned Kanban board where I can see tasks march across zones day by day and know their status at a glance (Figure 12.1).

You can create virtual Kanban boards in Jira or ADO, use task trackers like Trello, Hansoft, and Basecamp to stay on top of deadline, or simply visualize a milestone plan in Miro. Every lead figures out their own system, so experiment until you find what works best for you.

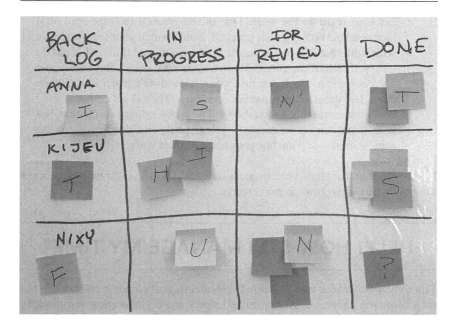

FIGURE 12.1   A typical Kanban board layout.

HOW DO I MANAGE A TEAM?

I joke that my leadership philosophy is to remember what my bad leads did and do the exact opposite. But avoiding their pitfalls only gets you so far. Being a good lead takes constant effort, humility, and willingness to admit you don't have all the answers. Above all, remember that your team defines your purpose. You're there to help them do their best work. That's the job. Here's what that means:

- Make sure they have enough work to do. And that they're challenged by it.
- Help them become better writers. That means feedback and leading by example, but it also means focused craft mentorship. Sign your team up for outside courses, craft books, and narrative talks. Ask the studio to reimburse training days. Find out your writers' personal goals and help them hit them.

- Let your team do the work. One of the greatest temptations you'll face as a lead is doing it all yourself. You'll watch your team struggle with work that still doesn't quite hit the mark, and think, "I could do it myself in half the time." Yes, you probably could. But then you'd *always* have to do it because your team didn't learn how. Teach them. Let them make mistakes and learn. They'll get better!
- Give them structure and stability. The project might be chaotic, but your team can be an oasis. Set clear goals and deadlines, reward achievements, and anchor your team in their work.

If your team understands your expectations and knows you'll help them meet them, they're on target to do good work.

HELP! HOW DO I MANAGE MY TIME?

I thought my calendar was so stuffed with meetings it couldn't get worse—but then came the pandemic. Meetings and syncs and collaboration and nitpicky tasks will eat your life away if you let them. There's always more work to do than there's time to do it, and trying to fit it all in can get overwhelming. But you don't need time travel to deal with it all, I promise.

Prioritize

What's on fire? What has to be done *right now* because it's blocking other teams? Sort your tasks by urgency. Enlist a producer to help you triage them and come up with a plan of attack. They love this stuff!

Assess & Adapt

Go down the list and see if you can simplify any tasks. What's the problem you're trying to solve with each one? What's the MVP[1] version of the task?

Delegate

Aaand we're back to good leadership. *Let your team do the work.* If they can't do it, pass it to another discipline or codev.[2] Outsource it! (Careful with those last two. You want to maintain oversight of your work.) Get comfortable with delegation or burn out trying to do it all. Those are your choices.

HOW DO I BALANCE CREATIVITY AND MANAGEMENT?

Every lead I know has the same struggle: How do I find time for creative work when there's so much other work to do? It's not easy, but it's important for your well-being. The happiest leads have a manage/create ratio of about 60/40. If less than 40% of your job is creative work, it can start to feel like drudgery. So how do you stay creative when there's so much administrative work to do? Honestly? Let it go. Be okay with administrative work falling off your plate to clear time for creative work. Book meetings with yourself for uninterrupted creative time. (Outlook has the Focus Time feature that will do it for you.) Talk to the studio about having what I call "story summits," full days off site or locked in a conference room to immerse yourself in creative work. And make sure that there's one little piece of the game you can call your own—even if it's just a series of in-game notes. Even if it's just one NPC. Fight for that creative outlet.

HOW DO I KEEP UP TEAM MORALE?

You'll be surprised how much of your job centers around team morale. Working on projects that span anywhere from 2 to 10 years means a whole lot of life happens in the space between. There will be project low points like major feature changes or inevitable downscoping.[3] You'll kill your darlings and shoot your babies in the crib. (Why are writing metaphors so violent?) The transition from prepro to production is usually a time of turmoil, as ideas that lived on paper fall apart when you action them. Stay positive, but stay honest with your team. If you've built a relationship of trust, they'll know you're being straight with them. You don't have to be Mary Sunshine, but don't catastrophize either. Here's some honesty:

- "We hoped to have this group of NPCs in our game, but we can't. I think they're an important part of the story, so it would've been nice."

And here's how to refocus your team's interest and keep them looking ahead:

- "With that faction gone, these other NPCs have to do some of the missing narrative work. Let's brainstorm..."

Perversely, these moments of narrative crisis can bring your team together. You'll brainstorm solutions together and learn to love the game all over again.

CUTS AND DOWNSCOPING

Scoping down is a necessary—and usually healthy—part of the development process, as you streamline the game into its critical elements. Cuts only become a problem when they're extreme, they happen frequently, or when essential game features get stripped out without reasonable justification. Downscoping has a big impact on narrative, tearing holes in our delicate spiderweb of storytelling. Always revisit your story and realign it with the new structure.

HOW DO I HELP MY TEAM THROUGH CRUNCH?

Try everything to avoid crunch. Work with your leads and producers to come up with a plan, a fallback plan, a Plan C, and an emergency contingency plan to protect against the issues that lead to crunch. Bang the drum about the evils of crunch. Be That Person. But if every contingency plan fails and crunch looms, here's how you can help your team.

- Talk to your writers about their individual needs and concerns.
- Strategize *as a team* for ways to reduce work or simplify tasks.
- Be flexible about crunch hours. If someone needs to pick up their kids, let them make that time up another day.
- Defend your team if they decide not to crunch.

Narrative's crunch is often invisible because it comes before everyone else's. While other teams are lazing through prepro, we're crunching. When they're crunching, we're polishing our work and looking ahead to DLC. It can look like writers are leaving early when the rest of the team is staying late. Make sure you raise the visibility of your team's hard work:

- Be ostentatious about your team's deliverables and deadlines. I get up in people's faces about the fact that my team is crunching when nobody else is. Keep it funny, keep it light, and don't point any fingers, but make your point.
- Narrative is the canary in the coalmine. If we're crunching now, they'll be crunching later. Raise a red flag for project leadership.

- Propose cuts. Better to lose lines than your health.
- Work more efficiently. Get your producers involved to find faster ways of working.

Basically, do whatever is necessary to lighten the load, shorten crunchtime, accommodate your team's needs, and let leadership know you're all badasses.

HOW DO I RUN A WRITER'S ROOM?

You've likely worked in a writing room by now, so you're familiar with what that process looks like. If not, it looks like this:

- **A goal.** A question to answer, story to break down, or specific topic to discuss.
- **A leader** who runs the meeting and keeps the discussion on track.
- **A notetaker** who writes it all down.
- **A flat hierarchy.** A good idea can come from anywhere and junior writers must be empowered to challenge leads and directors.

That last point is crucial! Creativity comes from safety. If you want your team to take creative risks, make it safe for them to do so. Encourage them to push for a better idea, the unusual twist, the untold story. It's *your* responsibility as lead to create an atmosphere where people can speak openly about deeply personal issues without fear of being mocked, put down, shamed, or any other negative reaction. Give your team that safety and they'll give you their best ideas.

You'll emerge from the writer's room with a "broken" story and individual tasks for the team. Give clear instructions and assignments. Set some deadlines. Then go your separate ways to write.

NOTES

1   MVP = Minimum viable product. The simplest version of something. The baseline version.
2   Codev = codevelopment team. Another studio that is working on the same project with you. Ubisoft has several studios that exclusively do codev work.
3   To "downscope" means trimming the game, usually by cutting features or diminishing their complexity. It reduces the scale of the game.

Making the Team

13

Here you are, on the other side of the hiring process at last! Feels strange, right? You'll get used to it, trust me. And you'll realize that hiring a solid, skilled team is far more complicated than simply picking the most experienced applicants. How many writers should you hire? When should you bring them on the project? How do you vet their samples and writing tests? Don't worry, folks, I gotcha!

HOW DO I PUT TOGETHER A TEAM?

Assembling your dream team is one of the great joys of leadership. Just ask Nick Fury. If you're lucky, you'll handpick people with talents you're excited to nurture. But there's more to building a team than posting an ad and selecting the most experienced writers. Before you get to that hiring point, you have to consider a host of project needs: the roadmap, your schedule, and the budget. (Always the budget. Always.)

Assess Your Needs

Your first step is to determine the narrative needs of the project. This means breaking it down by scope, schedule, and skills.

- **Scope**: Now's the time to estimate your line count. This shows how much writing your team needs to do. Break it down by type to get a workload estimate in the form of specific tasks and features, for example, "50 journal pages x 25 lines each."

DOI: 10.1201/9781003282259-14

- **Schedule**: Look at the project roadmap. Count backward from your final Localization handoff (not your ship date!) to see how much time you have to complete the work. How fast does your current team (or you) produce work? At that writing rate, how many people would you need to get all the work done on time? (Get a producer to help you timebox it. It's what they do!) This gives you a staffing estimate, for example, "four writers and an ND."
- **Skills**: Determine what abilities the work requires. Is it mostly barks? Do you need someone to create narrative systems and features? What skills do your team already have? What abilities are missing? This exercise gives you a list of skills and requirements, like the one in job posts.

Make a Hiring Plan

Now, assemble the information you've gathered into a hiring plan. It'll look something like "to do X amount of work at Y rate in Z time, I'll need W writers who have the following skills..."

Once you know what you need, meet with your lead and producer to review it and figure out a hiring schedule.

- Break those skill needs out into roles. "We'd need two mid-level writers and a narrative designer to do that amount of work that fast." Consider alternatives to hiring, such as a codevelopment studio or outsourced work.
- Production will help you figure out when to bring the writers on and will cross-reference your needs with the budget. (Always the budget.) This is your hiring schedule. "We'll hire a senior ND in the spring, a mid-level writer next summer," etc.
- Meet with Recruitment to review your needs and discuss the job requirements. Give them your role requirements. And there it is! A job post.

Once applications start rolling in, you'll end up adjusting the needs of each role. Say you interview a writer who doesn't have the required studio experience, but they're so talented you bring them on anyway. You'll have to tweak the remaining roles so that studio experience becomes a more important requirement. But generally, you'll be spoiled for choice. The hardest part of hiring is having to turn down brilliant candidates because it's the wrong project for them or because you already hired someone equally brilliant. You can't hire every great writer.

WHAT DO I DO AS A HIRING MANAGER?

Once you slap the job post on the website, the hiring process begins in earnest. Now it's your turn to ask the questions during interviews! In AAA, your recruiter does the heavy lifting of filtering applications. I like to sit down and chat through the role before posting, so recruiters understand what I'm looking for and what my timeframe is. They'll dig through the slush pile and send any interesting prospects your way. They have thousands of applications to sift through, so be patient!

- The recruiter flags promising candidates in Taleo, Jobvite, or whatever hiring program you use. You'll receive the application materials: resume, cover letter, and samples (if any) along with a hopeful "What do you think?" from the recruiter.
- Look over the materials and decide if you want to know more. The next step is up to you. You can chat with the candidate, ask for more samples, send them straight to the writing test—whatever you think is best.
- I'll show you how to create a writing test in a bit, but here's the important part: test for the skills your project needs. Don't test for screenwriting if your game is 95% systemic writing.
- Tell the recruiter if it's a yes or no, and what you want to do next. If it's a no, the recruiter will handle the rejection. If it's a yes, then you'll embark on the full hiring process—likely the same one you went through to get your job.

Be Fair

- Check with your studio for training to avoid unconscious bias in hiring and interviewing. Get diverse eyes on every application.
- Looking for "chemistry" or "culture fit" can lead to hiring homogeny, so be careful! That said, hire someone your team wants to work with. Ideally, they'll bring a fresh perspective or new skills to the existing team, but you want that electric buzz of synergy.
- Other disciplines should interview writers. They'll work with them too!
- Hiring can be a frustrating process for everyone involved, so approach it with empathy and diplomacy. Remember how it felt to be that nervous writer in the interview.

NEPOTISM AND CRONYISM

As tempting as it is to hire all your buddies, don't do it. You need the right people for the existing team and project. Your friend might not fit the project or there might be stronger candidates. It's fine to recommend friends or personally hand in their resumes. Most AAA companies offer rewards if they hire someone you recommended. Many have special "rec links"[1] for your friends. But be fair! When my friends are up for roles, I recuse myself from the process. I'll still recommend them, but I want everyone—including them!—to know they got the job on their own merits.

WHAT IF I DON'T HAVE BUDGET FOR WRITERS?

You'll often hear that AAA games are "carved from gold" because we have extravagant bankrolls and access to resources that many smaller studios don't. But we still have monetary constraints. Need a team of ten writers? Too bad! You only have budget for five, so adjust your hiring plan. You'll have to get creative. Maybe there's no need to hire full-time writers? Break down the work by task or by short writing sprints and spend your budget in small increments. Hire a contractor to write all your combat barks. Hire a freelance writer for a few weeks before recording sessions. (Some of the top writing talent in our industry does "mercenary work" on AAA projects.) Hire writers for brief, onsite workshops or pay them for small, specialized assignments. You can always outsource some work to narrative companies (Keywords, Talespinners, Martian Brothel, Sweet Baby Inc, etc.) or bring on codev. If you break down the game into tasks or features rather than time, it's easier to know where to invest your budget.

HOW DO I CREATE A WRITING TEST?

I bet you took a writing test to get where you are, so you know what they're like. But writing tests aren't one-size-fits-all. Design your test to screen for the specific skills and writing types your project needs. Don't ask applicants to write a screenplay if they're only writing systemic dialogue. Don't ask for branching dialogue if your game doesn't support branching. This seems obvious, but let me tell ya, friends, it's not. Create a test prompt that aligns with your project's needs. But keep it short! Respect the applicants' time—and your own. You're the one who has to review them all, remember?

THE INGREDIENTS OF A WRITING TEST

Include the following elements:

- The instructions for taking the test. "No more than 2–3 pages, screenplay format, etc."
- A deadline. One week, three days, whenever.
- The brief ("Write 2 character bios and a scene that contains them. The scene should contain the following...etc.")
- Instructions for returning it. ("Save in a pdf and return to the recruiter.")
- Something that lets them know to ask questions if they don't understand. Make it cheerful and encouraging so they're not afraid to ask.

Be Cool

Remember how it felt to interview for a job when you were first starting out? How intimidating the whole process feels? Yes? Then don't be a jerk in interviews. Don't create monstrous writing or design tests that waste candidates' time. Give applicants a fair chance when you're reading writing tests. You might only have a few stolen moments between meetings to look at resumes and read through tests, I get that. But remember what it felt like to pour your heart into a test for a job you really wanted and give each test your full attention and fair consideration. Also, "good" writing is subjective and every manager has different taste, so get a bunch of different eyes on candidates' work. Make decisions based on consensus, not personal preferences.

You might decide that you don't need to offer a writing test. If the writer or designer has experience and you know their work is good, why put them through that process just to tick a box? Alternatively, you could treat the test as a short contract and pay writers for a limited amount of work.

HOW DO I ONBOARD NEW WRITERS?

Once you've hired your amazing team, you'll need to onboard them and get them set up for success. Follow your company's standard processes, but make sure they also have the narrative-specific info they need. Give them a buddy to shadow for training in the day-to-day. Introduce them to key contacts on other teams. Give them a structured schedule and clear goals to meet. Do all the things you wanted done for you when you started. That will always be your touchstone: remembering how it was for you and fixing the problems you had back then.

HOW DO I ESTIMATE A LINE COUNT?

The earlier you do a line count, the less accurate it will be. That said, for budgeting reasons, you'll be asked to give a rough estimate in prepro before you know the shape of the story or how it'll be delivered. There are two ways to estimate the numbers: quick and dirty or napkin math.

Quick and Dirty

The easy way to get a count is to look at your comp set[2] of games. If your game has a sprawling world with a big main story and tons of activities and sidequests, compare it to *Horizon Zero Dawn* or *Assassin's Creed: Odyssey*. If it's a smaller, tighter game with deep buckets of systemic dialogue, then look to something like *Hades*. Do some digging around online to see if you can find line counts for the competitive game. *Hades*, for example, has over 300,000 words, two-thirds of which are dialogue.[3] Look at your tools to see how long *your game's* average line of dialogue is, do some math, and you've got your line count. Getting these numbers is even easier if you belong to a network of studios, such as Ubisoft. You're making a game roughly the size of *Watch Dogs*? Ping Ubi Montreal to get exact line count numbers straight from the source.

Napkin Math

If you can't get your mitts on any comp-set numbers, you'll have to math it out. Don't try it alone! Lasso folks from Audio and Production and get to work. You'll need to calculate three figures: quest lines, systemic lines, and text.

- **Quests (or missions)** – Cinematics live here, along with any bespoke lines of dialogue and text. Give the quests T-shirt sizes (S, M, L, XL) and assign a number to each size, like "a medium quest has 100 lines." Add it all up and note the number. It'll be smaller than you think!
- **Systemic** – This is usually the bulk of your games Greets, barks, combat lines, etc. The tricky part here is accounting for variants and voices if it's VO. Two enemy NPCs with ten bark prompts each isn't (necessarily) 20 lines. It might look more like 2 NPCS x (10 prompts x 5 variants) x 2 genders = 200 lines. It adds up fast!
- **Text** – These are less important to get right than voiced lines, but there are still massive amounts of items, menus, notes, journals, books etc. that your team will have to scribble out. I guess at numbers per region and then multiply by total regions. UI text is a shot in the dark.

If you put it all together, you could get a line count estimate that looks something like Table 13.1.

TABLE 13.1 A line count estimate in preproduction

TYPE	VOICED	UNVOICED	TOTAL (IN LINES)[a]
Quests	2,334	85	2,419
Systemic	47,500	3,126	50,626
Text	n/a	9,766	9,766
TOTAL	**49,834**	**12,892**	**62,811**

[a] I picked numbers *completely* at random to illustrate my point, so don't use them as a guide!

This will give you an accurate enough count to make a hiring plan, schedule VO sessions, and create a roadmap for your team's deliverables. When you enter production and have a clear picture of your story and narrative elements, do another estimate—this time with *real* numbers.

NOTES

1   Rec link = a form flags a candidate as your recommendation and keeps their application out of the slush pile.
2   Competitive set = The games most like yours in scale, production values, genre, etc. Your competitors.
3   Donnellan, Jimmy. "Supergiant's Hades Contains More Words Than The Iliad and Odyssey Combined." https://culturedvultures.com/supergiant-hades-word-count-dialogue/

Document
Everything

14

WHAT IS NARRATIVE DRIFT?

Have you ever noticed something in a game—a character, a conversation, a quest—that feels off tone or out of place in the world? Odds are that narrative drift caused it. Narrative drift happens when the team is working with outdated story information. That means that, say, a designer builds a level to explore Character Zed's childhood trauma, only to learn that Zed was redesigned as happy-go-lucky and there's no need for the level at all. Misalignments like this can mean weeks or even months of wasted work, which leads to burnout-causing churn and detachment. It's infuriating and dispiriting for everyone involved. When you realize the problem too late to change the misaligned work, it ends up in the game and players notice. Drift is an ever-present danger on large projects, especially multi-studio AAA games that span several time zones and languages.

HOW DO I PREVENT NARRATIVE DRIFT?

So how do you keep everyone on a sprawling team up to date with changes to story, lore, and other narrative elements? The answer is communication. Clear, concise communication. And because you're talking to disciplines that might not care much about narrative, you'd better be interesting. Good thing we're game writers! Edutainment is our jam.

Speak Their Language

We're writers, so we love words. Nobody loves words like we do. *Nobody*. That means nobody is going to read that wall-of-text email you sent out describing

DOI: 10.1201/9781003282259-15

the story changes. Nobody is going to read that gigantic story info-dump you just put on confluence. You have to find creative ways to get people's attention. Before reaching out, make sure you know two things:

- Who needs to know this information (Concept Art, the publisher, the general public)
- How to talk to them (images, spreadsheets, a face-to-face chat, etc.)

Once you know that, you can reach out to people in ways that speak to them. Use guerrilla tactics. Here are some methods I've tried over the years:

- **Wikis**: Everybody loves a good story, so make your routine documentation interesting and inviting. Share links to it often. Put "tl;dr" summaries at the top of each page.
- **Newsletters**: Your team's latest work delivered hot and fresh to everyone's inbox. Mmm, story!
- **Presentations and Talks**: Give a short presentation about it to the whole team. Make it funny if you can. Grab some pictures from Concept Art to make it pretty.
- **Open Office Hours**: Set aside time for a regular "story hour." Make sure everyone knows that your sole purpose during that time is to answer their questions and mean it. That short, monthly meeting will save you hours of time otherwise lost to emails.
- **Liaisons**: Send out your team as liaisons to other disciplines. Honestly, the most effective way to communicate is to explain face to face.
- **Signs, posters, ravens, telekinesis**: Hey, my notorious "It's been _0_ days since someone mentioned the Hero's Journey" sign has an actual purpose! I use it to engage people in discussions about our craft and help them understand that there's a lot they don't know about it. Then we can discuss how they prefer getting updates. Be open to whatever suggestions they make, within reason. (So, maybe no ravens after all.)

WHAT DOCUMENTATION DO I NEED?

Every project is different, but you should be looking at documents that fulfill three basic needs (Table 14.1).

TABLE 14.1   Types of narrative documentation for preproduction

REFERENCE	COMMUNICATION	AUDIENCE
Keep your team on target: lore wikis, character bios, internal style guides, story synopsis and treatments, discipline roadmaps, task schedules, and line count.	Prevent narrative drift with other disciplines. Docs such as your story bible, pitches, paper prototypes, and newsletters.	Redacted documents for an outside audience: job posts, writing tests, outsource and codev "packets."

Be careful with any documentation that goes outside your immediate team! The golden rule is "never share anything you wouldn't want players to see." Rework and redact as needed.

The type of documentation you need varies depending on where you are in development. In the Ideation stage, you'll write dozens of pitches and story synopses. In late production, you'll write all the text and readables you put off until the end, along with lines of voiced dialogue for last-minute VO pickup sessions. By that stage, the game should be completely written. If not, your only options are a massive Day One patch or delaying release. You don't want either of those options, trust me.

WHAT DO I NEED FOR PREPRODUCTION?

The documents you write during preproduction should lay the foundations of the game. If it's a sequel, you'll inherit a world and lore from previous projects and need to expand on it within set parameters. But sometimes you're lucky and you get to dream a new world into being.

Defining the World

If you're given a blank canvas, your first step is to define the game's universe and how different systems will express it. This worldbuilding stage is my personal favorite. It's pure, limitless possibility. If you can define these rules clearly, players will experience the world as cohesive and real, even if you never tell them what the rules are. Whether you start with a story or systems, you have to collaborate with other disciplines to make sure you're creating the universe holistically. If they want a brawler and your story's key is nurture, you'll have a challenge getting those ideas to work cohesively. Or the story might feel like a "wrapper" for unrelated gameplay.

Lay a Solid Foundation

The prepro flow varies from project to project, but you'll likely pitch "big picture" story ideas and outline major plot moments. Now is when you write the game's foundational documents: biographies for the key characters and lore for creatures and regions (the story bible), and descriptive briefs for Concept Art. Here are some narrative deliverables[1] for the prepro phase of a game:

- **Story Pitches**: These are sweeping, high-level pitches for the entire game story. You'll also pitch regional storylines, key characters and themes, and stylistic elements like genre, tone, and narrative devices.
- **Story Synopsis and Treatment**: The synopsis is a short summary of the story, usually only a few pages long. And the story treatment is a more detailed version of the synopsis. Eventually, these documents will become a scene breakdown or macro.[2]
- **Story Bible**: An overview of the Big Ideas for the entire game.
- **Character Biographies and Maps**: Character bios explain who the character is, define their backstory and personality, and offer a guide for how they behave and sound. Maps detail the character's arc at each point of the story. You'll turn these docs into casting briefs for actors later on.
- **Prototypes**: You'll collaborate with other teams on this work. It involves creating the narrative tools and delivery systems for the game, determining what "verbs"[3] your story will have, and generally supporting other teams with their prepro work.

Every project is unique, and every game has different deliverables. Preproduction involves *far* more work than I can list here, but it all adds up to one end: laying the foundation of the game and ensuring everything's ready for the go-go-go work of production.

HOW DO I WRITE A GOOD STORY PITCH?

Throughout development, you'll pitch your ideas to leadership, publishers, partners—even your colleagues. Whether it's a one-sentence elevator pitch by the coffee machine or a PechaKucha-style PowerPoint presentation, your pitch has to sell your idea. You want to get people excited about it. Here's how you do that:

- **Know your audience**: Communicate in the way you know will reach them. Don't be afraid to try novel approaches. "Whatever works" is your motto.
- **Tell a story**: This is your gift! The dice are weighted in your favor. Entertain them, engross them, and keep them listening.
- **Images not words**: Don't write a long text-y screed. Your idea won't get through. If it's a presentation, put up one image per slide. Connect each image with your core idea.
- **Focus on what lights you up**: Passion is contagious. You're more persuasive when you believe in what you're pitching. Make your audience *care* about your idea.

HOW DO I WRITE A STORY BIBLE?

People are obsessed with story bibles. I've met so many young writers over the years who spoke dreamily about creating one someday. And they probably will! They might already have contributed to one. That's because story bibles are no longer massive tomes that lock one version of the game into unchanging text. Modern story bibles are living documents that change and grow with the project. They're searchable wikis, and the entire team contributes bits and pieces as the project trundles along. But even a fluid wiki has to start somewhere. And it usually falls to writers to assemble all the plans and ideas floating around in prepro, from every discipline, and bind those concepts to the page. Here's an example table of contents from a AAA story bible (Figure 14.1).

As you can see, it encompasses the whole game and gives the world its shape. It's also a one-stop reference for teams to see what other disciplines have planned. A good story bible also includes ideas for sequels, DLC, and

Story Bible   **MY SUPERCOOL GAME**   by Anna Megill

CONTENTS

OVERVIEW..X

THE WORLD...XX

GAME PILLARS...XX

NARRATIVE..XX

THEMES...XX

STORYTELLING METHODS..XX

TONE & LANGUAGE...XX

STORY SUMMARY..XX

CHARACTERS...XX

UNIQUE ITEMS..XX

WORLD EVENTS...XX

WORLD LOCATIONS...XX

GAMEPLAY..XX

COMBAT & ENEMIES..XX

ECONOMY...XX

MARKETING...XX

THE FUTURE...XX

REFERENCE MATERIALS..XX

FIGURE 14.1   Table of contents for a AAA story bible.

marketing. Keeping a detailed bible or wiki updated is a fulltime job though. The pages lose accuracy and relevance over time, and the game itself becomes "the source of truth" for all work. That's okay! Change is inevitable and good. After a certain stage, the bible serves as a snapshot of the project's past "pure" form to remind you of the original vision.

WHAT GOES IN A HOUSE STYLE GUIDE?

First, be aware that art has style guides that refer to the look of certain aspects the game. So call yours a *writing* style guide and you'll be good. It's tempting to write detailed instructions for every grammatical nuance of your game, but honestly, short and memorable is the best path here. Here are a few things to include in your style guide:

- **Editing style**: Make sure everyone is using the same grammar and punctuation rules from the start. It will save you trouble down the road. All the studios I've worked at use Chicago style, with CMoS as their primary style reference tool.
- **Instructions for tone**: Tone can be the trickiest part of game writing, especially if it's unusual or narrowly defined. I've written in several tones throughout my career: high fantasy, dystopian dark fantasy with hints of steampunk, and New Weird, to name a few. Give your writers guidelines to help them nail it and stay in sync.
- **Project-specific guidelines**: This is the nuts and bolts of the project's writing. The mechanical side of writing. Anything that explains the house rules for writing standard narrative elements should go here. Some examples:
  - Conversation trees should have 3–5 options.
  - In the open world, frontload ambient lines with critical information.
  - Journal entries must be 150–200 words from the player-character's POV.
- **Notes on game "culture"**: If groups of characters share a trait that affects their worldview or speech, mention it here. In *CONTROL*, we wanted office workers to treat supernatural phenomena not as extraordinary but as annoying and inconvenient. And we wanted to find some humor in those interactions.
- **A glossary**: Create this as you go along. Lob any unusual names or terms onto a confluence page with their pronunciation and where they're used. You'll use it for your own reference now and for use in the recording studio later. Legal will need to research your names and made-up terms for copyright infringement, so start that list early.

WHAT DO I NEED FOR PRODUCTION?

Your main focus during production is (surprise!) making the game so you can ship it. Documentation in this stage merely expands on work you started in prepro. Your character bios become casting briefs. Your story bible becomes design documents and a wiki. Pitches become playable missions. And your story treatments become a macro that breaks down the entire storyline into detailed beats.

You'll beef up your team with more hires, especially contractors, and bring on codevs or outsource partners. You'll need to plan your team's schedule and account for studio time. And you'll be in the studio for mocap and recording sessions, so you'll need documentation for those too. Here's a few of the documents you'll need (Table 14.2).

TABLE 14.2   Types of narrative documentation for production

REFERENCE	COMMUNICATION	AUDIENCE
Keep your team on target: theme and character trackers, narrative design maps, workflows, assignments, kanban boards, and folders of drafts and versions.	Prevent narrative drift with other disciplines. Docs such as your narrative wiki, design documents, macros, narrative feature specifications or "one pagers," and ongoing newsletters.	Redacted documents for an external audience: glossary and pronunciation guide, name lists (for approval), casting briefs, marketing copy, trailer and demo scripts, screenplays, ESRB/PEGI paperwork, and all writing for the game itself.

If you compare this table to the one for prepro, you'll see there's a shift in weight from internal documents to external deliverables. That's because all of the documentation leads to a singular output: a video game that you can release to the world.

HOW DO I KEEP TRACK OF THE STORY?

Once you hand off your story to other teams, it can quickly get hard to keep track of all the moving pieces. Especially as it fractals out into sidequests and associated gameplay elements. You can track work on features and track tasks in Jira or Shotgrid, but how do you visualize the story when it's that big and complicated? I discussed solutions for tracking tasks in Chapter 12, but you'll need to find new methods for mapping out and tracking all the narrative elements. Everybody has their own preferred method: a big wall of sticky notes, the macro aka the spreadsheet of doom, a Miro board, an untouchable whiteboard in a back room somewhere. Personally, I use maps with overlays for main quests, sidequests, character trajectories, and all the other narrative information that has a timeline. It helps me mentally walk the golden storyline through the world. But there's no one right way to do it, so try a few until you discover what works best for you.

HOW DO I PREP FOR RECORDING AND MOCAP SESSIONS?

A shining moment for game writers is seeing our funny little words brought to life by talented actors. Sitting in on mocap sessions is a joy. You'll occasionally be asked to direct sessions as a lead, but usually you get to kick back and answer infrequent questions about backstory, lore, and pronunciation. It's fun! But only if you have the answers to hand. Here's a high-level overview of materials to prepare before heading into the studio:

Schedule

Your work schedule and deadlines will be driven by recording sessions. Once you've booked a studio (months or even years in advance) and reserved a spot in an actor's schedule, it's a huge hassle to move those dates. Plan your team's deadlines and deliverables around them.

Casting Materials

Most AAA games start the casting process in prepro. That means you're casting roles that might change, flip gender, or get cut by the time a recording session comes around. These factors are out of your control, so make your best estimations and roll with the inevitable changes.

For casting, you'll need a brief character bio and short script. Some studios prefer a monologue to let actors really stretch out and show their chops. Some studios prefer a short dialogue to see how actors work with each other. Some studios like both. Regardless of the format, keep those materials to about a page apiece.

Scene Counts

If it's too early to do a line count for the role, you can probably estimate a scene count. Exactly what it says on the tin: count how many times a character appears in your story. From that you can give a finger-in the-air estimate of how much studio time you'll need for that actor.

Glossary

If your game has a bunch of made-up words or names, then you should provide a glossary for studio use. I start this document way in advance, even if it's just a confluence page with a list of names, and add to it as we go along. Some studios record VO of each word as a pronunciation guide for actors. Schmancy!

Represent!

Make sure a writer is in every recording session. This will primarily be seniors or leads, but it's best to have the person who did the writing present when it's recorded. It's also useful for juniors to see how pages become performance and what trips up a reading. It might be the first time they've ever seen their words come alive, so find ways for them to experience that magic.

HOW MUCH STUDIO TIME DO I BOOK?

Don't figure this out on your own! Grab a producer, examine the scene count per actor, and work up some estimates together. Keep these points in mind:

- You must book actors for a minimum rate and time (usually four hours, per SAG-AFTRA rules).
- Actors work at different speeds. Experienced pros can churn out ninety flawless barks an hour, while novices might struggle to give a good read on thirty.
- The rule of thumb for screenplays is one page = one minute. In reality, mocap time varies wildly depending on factors like the ratio of action to dialogue.

- If the script requires lots of yelling or screaming, you'll tear up the actor's voice after a while. Be kind. Book their time with that consideration in mind.
- You get better performances from actors who can play off each other. Having an actor read alone in the booth works fine for barks, but plan on rehearsals and group studio time for any high-end cinematics or emotional scenes. This means coordinating very busy schedules to get everyone together. It's hard, but absolutely worth it.

Toward the end of AAA projects, recording sessions run in several studios at once. And no matter how much time you allocate, it always takes longer than you think. The story will change so you'll have to re-capture some scenes. That's what pickup sessions are for. I hope you built a juicy buffer into your line count estimate!

HOW DO I HELP LOCALIZATION?

The documentation you create for casting will live again with Loc. Especially your glossary. Make one writer your dedicated Loc contact. Empower them to triage all localization questions and dispense them to appropriate departments. They should also compile the questions into a FAQ for Loc's reference. That prevents endless pings for repeat questions like "What gender is your character HOOTIN NANNY?"

NOTES

1   Deliverables are the work you hand over at the end of certain time period, like a sprint or milestone. For narrative these are usually concrete documents like screenplays and spreadsheets of barks.
2   A "macro" is a detailed blockout of all questlines and missions. It contains plot, character arcs, gameplay, cinematic types, and other narrative needs. It's often a massive spreadsheet that updates regularly.
3   Verbs = gameplay actions. What players can do to express story. Common verbs: walk, talk, find, fight.

Exit Stage Right

15

WHEN SHOULD I LEAVE A JOB?

You're happy at your job, but sometimes you wonder what else is out there. Or maybe you're frustrated that a promised raise or promotion never quiiite arrives. Or maybe you're just bored. People switch jobs for countless reasons. During the pandemic, I couldn't go online without seeing someone announce a new role. It felt like the entire industry got reshuffled. So if you peek over the fence at the greener grass of new opportunities, you're not alone! But is it worth the risk? *In this economy?* To find out, ask yourself these questions:

- Are you doing work you care about?
- Are you being paid the wage you want?
- Do you have opportunities to grow?
- Are you getting what you want from your career (recognition, creative satisfaction, etc.)?

If you answer no to any of these questions, then see what else is out there. Looking isn't leaving! It's merely exploring your options.

HOW DO I LOOK FOR WORK WHILE WORKING?

Carefully! Most employers aren't thrilled to know you're looking for work elsewhere, so why tell them? Schedule interviews for lunch hours and after

DOI: 10.1201/9781003282259-16

work, and give recruiters your personal email. If your search doesn't affect your performance in any way, your studio won't even know you're looking.

Start the Hunt

Finding a job in the industry is much easier from the inside. If you've kept up a healthy network, you'll find that recruiters ping you with possibilities, friends tell you about roles at their studio, opportunities bubble up everywhere. I have a personal rule to always respond to recruiters and have that initial, exploratory chat. Always. It's exciting to see what projects are in development and you get to meet cool new people. Most of the time, the job isn't for you and you'll return to work with your FOMO satisfied. But you never know! Maybe they're making your dream project, the one you'd forever regret missing out on. It's worth finding out.

To start your job hunt, go back to Chapter 3 and follow the steps there. And, just to be safe, revisit the noncompete clauses in your contract. Stay on the right side of your agreement.

HOW DO I SHOW WORK THAT'S UNDER NDA?

You don't. Unless your studio gives explicit permission to share it, which is unlikely, you're violating your NDA. I'm not saying that people don't do it. I've seen work in portfolios from unpublished projects. (Some work is still stamped "CONFIDENTIAL"!) All that does is scream "I'm untrustworthy!" at future employers. And it means legal trouble if the work gets traced back to you. Don't do it. It's not worth it. Instead, explain that you can't show work from a current project because it's under NDA. Studios will understand. Really! It happens all the time. They know how it is. Show work from published projects, or talk about your current work in an abstract way.

- **Bad**: "I'm currently designing some journal entries for the shooter I'm working on. They appear on wall screens in the central hub of a space center."
- **Good**: "On an earlier project, I designed journal entries that revealed the character's inner monologue and reinforced the subtext of their relationships."

For samples, fill your portfolio with work from other projects or write custom pieces in a similar style to your current project. Check back to Chapter 6 if you want help anonymizing the work and ensuring you don't violate your NDA.

If you need personal references and you trust them, confide in your lead or a senior team member. Or see if a former colleague will vouch for you. But it's safest to say, "My current company doesn't know I'm looking." I hear that a lot as a hiring manager. It opens the door to conversations about why you're leaving and what you're looking for in the new job. As long as you don't badmouth your current company, honesty helps you and the new company align on your hopes and expectations.

WHAT IF I DON'T WANT THE JOB OFFER?

Don't take it. "Just looking" at other projects is fine. But if you decide the job's not for you, don't toss that offer in the bin! It's leverage. Go talk to your lead. Tell them you have an offer (don't say you don't want it!) and discuss your options. Now's the time to push for a raise or that never-arriving promotion or more ownership of story features. It's a well-known industry truth that the fastest way to increase your salary is by hopping studios—use that fact to your advantage. See if your studio's willing to make the changes you need. If they're happy with your work, most places will try to match the offer. Whatever you agree on, get it in writing. If they call your bluff and won't (or can't) give you what you want, then you have to choose: stay or go. If you stay, be aware that this failed negotiation might haunt you. The company won't take your threats to leave seriously after this.

I WANT THIS JOB OFFER! NOW WHAT?

Congrats! It's exhilarating to get a job offer, especially when it's a step up. But before you agree to anything, check your contract for the notice period clause. How much notice do you have to give? In the US, with at-will contracts, it's usually 2–6 weeks. In Europe, it's not unusual to see notice periods of 3–6 months, especially for hard-to-fill senior roles. Mark the language around the notice period to make sure you understand the requirements. Try to answer these questions:

- When do you have to give notice?
- Who do you give notice to? (Your lead, HR, somebody else?)
- Do you have to give notice in writing?
- Do they need to sign off before it's official? (This is important!)
- Are there any penalties incurred by your leaving? For example, the company might require you to repay a percentage of your relocation costs if you leave within the first year.

Make sure you understand *exactly* what leaving means for you. The fees and penalties can be daunting, by design. See if your new employer will pay for them (signing bonuses are good for covering these fees). If not, decide if it's still worth it.

Timeline

Next, you should plan your timeline. My formula for job hunting is "however long you think it will take to get to the contract-signing point" *plus* the time of your notice. Add extra time for relocation. Here's what that might look like.

TIME TO CONTRACT	NOTICE PERIOD	RELOCATION TIME	TOTAL
1 month +	3 months +	2 months	= 6 months

Six months might seem like an absurd amount of time to plan for, but I've had it take longer than that. If you're moving overseas, you're at the whims of the visa-approval process. Or you could spend six months looking for work and waiting for the right project to come along. Plan for the worst-case scenario and budget your time carefully. If you're lucky, it'll go fast. You could sign the contract tomorrow, have your studio waive the notice period, and go to work next week at a studio down the street. You never know.

HOW DO I LEAVE ON GOOD TERMS?

I've seen people burn all their bridges on their way out the door. Some people try to burn down the whole studio. Yet, it's so easy to leave on good terms.

If you're giving reasonable notice and not violating your NDA or contract, you have nothing to worry about. In some worst-case scenarios where you're fired or fleeing a toxic job, etiquette isn't top of your mind, I get that. In those cases, you probably don't care if you torch everything in your path. But those extreme cases aside, try to leave a studio amicably. Game devs come and go from the same studio many times in their career. You night work at one company, leave for another project, then come back when you're done. The game-writing world is small and you want to keep as many options open as you can. You never know what the future holds.

HOW DO I RESIGN?

Check your contract for notice period requirements. Most places ask that you resign *in writing* a certain number of weeks or months before leaving. If your resignation isn't official until they sign the paperwork, get it out asap. It sometimes takes a week or two to get it back and that's time added on to your official notice period. Know who to address and where to send the letter, and you're set.

HOW DO I WRITE A RESIGNATION LETTER?

My advice is to keep it short and straightforward. Include only necessary information.

- Your name
- The date
- The name of the person you're giving notice to. (Studio name is fine.)
- The purpose of the letter
- Your notice period
- Your signature (or typed name)

That's it. No frills, no meandering explanations. You can include a nice nod to your experience at the company or an acknowledgment of why you're leaving, but keep it brief. If you're quitting unhappy, you'll be tempted to vent and point fingers in the letter. Don't do it. Save it for your exit interview, when feedback is welcome. Keep it professional. Here's a standard resignation letter.

September 1, 2023
Dear Textbox Studios,

I'm writing to submit my resignation from my role as Scriptwriter. After much consideration, I've accepted a job at another game studio. My last day of work will be at the end of my three-months' notice, on December 1st.

Thank you for the opportunity to be part of your studio these past four years. I've enjoyed working at Textbox and getting to know the wonderful people here. I wish you all the best and hope the project is a great success.

Sincerely,
[YOUR NAME]

Not much to it, is there? If you're leaving because of abuse or harassment, mention it in your letter without going into detail. "I'm leaving because harassment has created an intolerable work environment for me." Imagine how you'd feel if the letter was read out loud in a court of law, and let that guide your wording.

HOW DO I GUARANTEE MY GAME CREDITS?

It's better to negotiate game credits when you're signing your contract, but if you didn't, lock them down now. In writing. Right now, the memory of your contributions is fresh in everyone's minds and they'll be more willing to negotiate. Once you're gone, it's a different beast. A million things could transpire before the game comes out. Your accomplishments might be forgotten. Don't risk it. Reach an agreement before you go. Be prepared for some pushback though! Some studios don't credit devs who leave before ship. Some offer a standard "special thanks" blanket credit. Try your best to change it to your earned credit, but if you can't, take the lesson and move on. Next time, you'll put it in your contract. And no matter what credit you receive, you can still list the correct credit on your resume.

WHAT WORK CAN I TAKE WITH ME?

Your resignation is the appropriate stage to lock down permissions for samples. Have discussions with your studio about what work you can—and absolutely can't—share. If they refuse to let you share anything, try to pry some concessions from them. What if you share work after the game releases? Can you share it if you scrub the serial numbers off? Work with them to reach a compromise. And again, get it in writing. It's easier to secure this now and in person than it will be three years down the road when nobody remembers your contributions. Also, be careful if you're downloading documents for your own records. Understand what your NDA covers and what you're free to take with you. You don't want to accidentally abscond with company secrets. Most companies lock you out of the system the moment you leave, so download your work before your last day.

SHOULD I SIGN ALL THESE PAPERS?

The United States has a new law that voids "gag order" clauses in cases of harassment or abuse. You don't have to stay silent to get severance pay. That's an exciting and gratifying development, but you should still be cautious when signing paperwork. And trust me, you'll have a mountain of paperwork to sign on the way out. Danger, danger, danger! If you negotiated hard with your contract, don't ruin it by signing away your rights now. Know every clause and article, and what their ramifications are. If it seems unreasonable or unfair, don't sign it. I mean, you're already leaving, right? They can't force you.

In most cases, the paperwork is pretty standard and straightforward. Most companies ask you to confirm your departure date and affirm you've returned your keycard, laptop, and other company property. If it looks like the resignation form pictured her (Figure 15.1), then sign away!

**Employee resignation
Confirmation**

Employer

Company	Organisational numer
Contact person	Phone

Employee resignation (filled by the employee)

Name	Social Security number
Date of resignation:	

Information (filled by the employee)

The employees (new) address:
The employees phone number The employees private email address:

Confirmation (filled by the employer)

Your last day of employment will be on: Your last day at work will be on:

Miscellaneous

Employee:	....	....	....
		signature	Place and date
HR:	....	....	....
		signature	Place and date

FIGURE 15.1   A standard resignation form.

WHAT DO I SAY IN MY EXIT INTERVIEW?

Goodbye? Your studio will likely have an exit interview with you. This is the appropriate forum for feedback and grievances. Recruiters expect it, and often request it. If you prefer to note your complaints in writing, email them your feedback after you leave. Some companies have long questionnaires or a standard Q&A they follow for legal reasons. Answer however you'd like, but again, keep it professional and don't torch that bridge. Who knows? You might want to return someday.

On the Road

16

Time to take your show on the road! Working abroad opens up a world of job opportunities, but relocation can be a logistical nightmare, even for seasoned travelers. Moving itself is enough of a challenge, but when you're leaving behind friends and family to build a new life in a country where you don't speak the language, the list of obstacles is overwhelming. I'd like to say, "It's easier than it seems," but unfortunately, it's not. I'll get you started with some tips, but you'll have to navigate a snarl of rules and dependencies to pull off an international move.

WHY CAN'T I WORK REMOTELY?

Maybe you can! Remote opportunities have exploded since the pandemic, so check to see if your favorite studio lists that as an option. If you don't see it explicitly called out in the job post, ask the recruiter during your initial screening. Why go through the entire hiring process only to discover they need you on site?

Reasons for Being Local

Studios don't make roles "onsite only" just to be mean. There are political and legal considerations behind their hiring decisions. Many governments offer tax breaks to companies who base their operations there. They might require studios to hire locals over international candidates. Companies like Bungie can only hire remote workers from certain US states, while other companies can only offer remote roles to independent contractors. If the company says it's a remote job, make sure you understand what "remote" means to them.

DOI: 10.1201/9781003282259-17

HOW DO I FIND INTERNATIONAL WORK?

It's easy to find jobs anywhere in the world now. All the job aggregators and boards in Chapter 3 list international roles too. Follow the same steps you would when applying for any other job. It can take longer to apply for international work, and cost a vault of money, so prepare yourself. Here are some key questions to ask recruiters during your initial interview:

- Is remote work an option for this job?
- Who qualifies for remote work?
- Does the studio pay for relocation?
- What does the typical relocation package include?
- How long does a typical relocation take?
- If I relocate, what type of visa does this job require?
- Does the studio have any requirements outside of the standard application process?

That last point is critical! Some studios require rigorous background checks that add months to your relocation time. Try to get an estimate (four weeks? two months?) so you can factor that into your relocation timeline. You don't want to give notice at your current job only to find out it'll be three months before your new job can officially hire you. Gather enough information to plan your move schedule.

HOW DO I PLAN FOR OVERSEAS WORK?

The moment you even *think* about relocating for work, jump online and research visa requirements. To work abroad, you'll need to prove your expertise. That proof is your education and employment history. A Special Expert visa, common for work in the EU and Nordics, will require higher education diplomas and past-job contracts. Same for an H-1B visa,[1] which is for skilled tech workers and game designers in the US. If you don't have the necessary education, then make up for it with equivalent work experience. That's harder than it sounds because of the "three for one" rule: for every year of college, you need three years of work experience.[2] If you don't have *any* higher education degree, you'll need at least twelve years of game-writing experience to qualify. Now you know why I encouraged you to get that college degree!

Visa requirements vary by country, but here are the standard asks:

- Passport
- Visa (right to work in the country)
- Diploma(s) or proof of relevant accreditation
- Proof of employment (from your company)
- Biometrics (fingerprints or retina scan)

Biometrics and visas require an appointment with your host country's embassy, and they're usually booked solid for months. To further complicate the process, some paperwork approvals are dependent on others. For example, you can't get a visa without a valid passport. That means you'll have to procure each item in a specific order and be mindful of varying deadlines. It takes time to scramble up all the required paperwork, so start early.

HOW DO I PAY FOR MY MOVE?

First off, *you* shouldn't pay for your move. Moving is hideously expensive, and you don't want to get stuck with that bill. If a company offers you a job, they should pay for your relocation. Be clear about that expectation from the start.

You'll negotiate your relocation package as part of your contract, but most companies have a standard package. Here are the basics they should provide.

• Visa fees	• Travel expenses
• Visa assistance agent	• Household moving
• Biometrics	• Temporary housing

Some companies give you a stipend—a big lump of money to spend however you want. Do some research ahead of your negotiations to check if it's enough. You might think a USD 5,000 stipend is plenty for one person, but it won't get you very far. Between visa costs, biometrics, moving expenses, flights, and unexpected fees (the UK asks you to pay for several years of NHS service upfront) your move could run anywhere from USD 5,000 to 10,000 for just one person! The more senior your role, the more generous your relocation package should be.

Don't forget, that list is the *basics*. The must-haves. You should also negotiate for some nice-to-haves: a translator to help set you up in the new country, pet travel fees, furniture and household items, a rental car, phone, and anything else that might help you start your new life. Haggle hard for your reloc package. Your new life depends on it!

HOW DO I APPLY FOR A VISA?

A visa is just a stamp that says you have permission to live and work in that country. But, oh, the hoops you'll jump through to get that stamp! Procuring a visa starts with you (or someone on your behalf) applying for one through the country's website. In the US, it's the State Department website. Read all the instructions, note the deadlines, then start gathering your paperwork. Fill out the forms and supply the necessary documentation (diplomas, travel history, proof of sponsorship from your company, etc.). Then wait for your approval to arrive.

Biometrics

As part of the visa process, you might be asked to submit biometrics. That's just a fancy way to say fingerprints and retina scan. You can only get this done at specific locations—usually the embassy or consulate—and you'll have to book an appointment in advance. This might mean traveling to that city and staying overnight. When you go to the appointment, make sure you have all the required paperwork at hand. They won't process your application or do your scans without it, and you'll have wasted the trip. Triple check that everything is in order.

Picking Up the Visa

This is where things can go south. There are some tricky timing issues associated with the visa—when you can enter the country, how long in advance you can apply for one, and how recently you've visited the region. You might get a temporary visa that allows you to enter the country and pick up your final visa once you arrive. Make sure you know exactly what to do and that you have all the necessary paperwork at each step. Trust me, you don't want to mess this up.

I know devs who've been turned away at the border, held in detention, and deported because they messed up their visa paperwork. If you've only lived in your own country, you can't imagine how tough other countries can make it to emigrate. Don't risk getting any detail wrong.

WHERE WILL I LIVE?

Your company should provide you with a place to stay. It's a deal-breaker if they don't. Most studios will offer some kind of temporary housing for relocated devs, and studios that relocate devs frequently might even have a permanent "dormitory." I've generally had good experiences with temporary housing, but some rooming situations are…less than ideal. Company quarters are meant to be short term, but that doesn't mean they should be gross. Remember that the relocation package isn't a favor; it's part of your remuneration. You have every right to complain about housing that is unclean or unsafe. In an extreme situation, go stay at a hotel and ask the company to reimburse you. But in most cases, your landing pad will be fine for a short stay.

CAN I BRING MY PETS?

Talk about a deal-breaker! Yes, of course your cuties should come with you. Negotiate their relocation along with your own, then brace yourself. Because if you thought your move was difficult and expensive, wait until you plan for your pets. There are stringent requirements for their travel—especially if you're relocating to another continent. You'll need a specific type of microchip, proof of negative rabies and titer tests, and a verified health certificate stamped within a few days of your trip. Airlines have strict rules about pets flying in cabins or in cargo, and they require crates that meet rigid standards. Plan ahead and know exactly how to get your pet into the new country smoothly. The last thing you want is to arrive, discover you're missing critical documentation, and have your pet put into quarantine. Some quarantine periods, such as Japan's, can last up to six months! Don't put your darlings through that.

HOW DO I CHOOSE A MOVER?

Check your reloc package to see what it covers. Does your company pay for movers? Is there a limit on what you can pack? If you're paying for movers, what's your budget? Once you know, ask the studio if you can talk to someone who moved internationally. They'll be a goldmine of tips about good movers, services, and a bunch of "learn from my mistakes!" stories.

If nobody recommends a mover, you'll have to pick your own. Be careful! If a price seems too good to be true, it probably is. Look for hidden costs like harbor fees, ship-to-door costs, and insurance. And expense isn't your only worry. International shipping is unsurprisingly riddled with scams and shady companies. It's better to spend a bit more and ship with reputable movers.

WHAT SHOULD I PACK?

If you have the budget for it, pack up your whole house. Why not? But usually, you'll need to mind costs and get rid of some belongings. I toss about two-thirds of my stuff every time I move. Lugging heavy furniture country to country doesn't make sense for me. There's no point taking electronics or appliances either, as countries have voltage differences. In fact, ditch all your mundane household items and buy new ones there. Embrace the spirit of adventure! You can always put treasured items in storage and have a friend ship them to you later. But honestly? You'll be surprised by how little you'll miss them.

DO I NEED TO SPEAK THE LANGUAGE?

No. You don't *have* to learn it. English is the common language on the floors of most AAA game studios, so you'll be able to make yourself understood. And you'll usually write the game in English. It's very easy to not learn the local language, but that's a huge mistake. Speaking the native tongue will help you understand your new culture better and expand your intellectual horizons. And boy, does it help at tax time! Gaining a new lens on language is an incredible opportunity for wordsmiths like us, so don't blow it just because English is easy.

HOW DO I HANDLE CULTURE SHOCK?

Nobody's immune to culture shock, not even jaded jetsetters like me. It can hit you at odd times and in surprising ways. My worst moment of culture shock was when I returned home to the US after living abroad for several years. I couldn't get over how foreign it felt. My own home! Every society has a host of unspoken rules and behaviors that we know so well they've become invisible. When you're in a new country, you'll bump up against those all the time without realizing it. That friction builds up and can hit you all at once.

The best cure for culture shock is to embrace the culture. That means engaging with it. Explore your new city. Learn the language. Make local friends. Don't live out of your suitcase! Unpack, get comfortable, and make a home for yourself. Put in the effort to build a new life. If you don't find ways to connect with your new culture, you won't last.

Change Your Mind

With all of its challenges, living abroad isn't for everyone. Some people are rooted in one place and love the security and familiarity that brings. Completely understandable! But if you're willing to take the leap, life abroad will change your lens on the world. You won't realize how much your perspective has changed until you go home and look at your old, familiar world with fresh eyes. The invisible veil of familiarity falls away and you see everything clearly again. That illumination is the great gift of traveling and living abroad.

HOW DO I NETWORK ABROAD?

If you move, you might get cut off from your network. They're in a different time zone, they're hanging out together at industry events, and you're alone in a far-off place (Figure 16.1). It's tough. It's important to keep in touch with these old friends and colleagues, but never fear, you'll make new ones. Here's your chance to spread a wider net in the industry and meet a new circle of contacts. Reach out to people at your new studio for introductions and attend local events. Find someone to show you around town. It's a fantastic way to meet new folks.

FIGURE 16.1 View from a porthole at the Hoek van Holland Harbor.

HOW DO I "FIND MY COMMUNITY"?

Living in another country is isolating, especially when you're the only one like you. A sense of belonging can be especially important for marginalized writers. Find a community of people who accept you. If you can't get the support you need through the studio, find it outside work. Take classes—art classes are great when you don't speak much of the language. Try bouldering or swimming if you're on the sporty side. Or join your local expat group. IGDA has branches throughout Europe and the Americas. Reach out to international groups for your marginalization: women's groups, gayming groups, and online mingles for game devs of color. Online meetups with groups like The GIG are great ways to be social and stay centered. And there are local writers' groups everywhere you go. The group doesn't matter as much as your shared interest and acceptance. If you can't connect with people and find acceptance in your new life, you won't last. Force yourself to step outside your comfort zone and meet people. Find a community to support you. This advice isn't just for living abroad; take it with you wherever you go in your career as a game writer. Friendships with your fellow writers and with the larger games development community will be your saving grace. Nobody will understand your highs, your lows, or your love for the medium the way they will. That shared bond, that feeling of community, makes the whole journey worthwhile.

NOTES

1   US Citizenship and Immigration Services. "O-1 Visa: Individuals with Extra-ordinary Ability or Achievement." Accessed 26 April 2023. https://www.uscis.gov/working-in-the-united-states/h-1b-specialty-occupations
2   Shihab & Associates. "Degree Equivalency & Work Experience." Accessed 28 April 2023. https://www.shihabimmigrationfirm.com/employment-based-immigration/h-1b-visas/degree-equivalency-work-experience/

Wrap It Up

17

Well, we did it! We made you into a game writer! Haha, of course becoming a writer isn't as simple as reading a handbook, but I hope that we made progress together and got you off to a good start. If you've read this book, you know more than I did in my first decade as a game writer. It's the best leg-up I can give you; I hope it helps.

You can always check out my *Guide* if you need more advice, but I also urge you to get out there into the world and start making games. Words are the foundation, but it's our very human experience that brings them to wondrous life. You need a rich life beyond the page to make a world worth living in. Games taught me that. And now I'm teaching you. It's been a joy sharing this pocket adventure with you. See you out there, friend.

DOI: 10.1201/9781003282259-18